Little Lost Girl   F
By Liesha Joseph

L. Sommers

LITTLE

GIRL

LOST

LITTLE GIRL LOST

One
Woman's
Journey
Beyond
Rape

Leisha Joseph

*with
Deborah
Bruner
Mendenhall*

DOUBLEDAY

*New York London
Toronto Sydney
Auckland*

PUBLISHED BY DOUBLEDAY
a division of Bantam Doubleday Dell Publishing Group, Inc.
1540 Broadway, New York, New York 10036

DOUBLEDAY and the portrayal of an anchor with a dolphin are trademarks of
Doubleday, a division of Bantam Doubleday Dell Publishing Group, Inc.

ISBN 0-385-49239-1

Book design by Deborah Kerner

TO YOU WHOSE
THRONE IS IN HEAVEN,
NOW BE GLORIFIED
THROUGH THE BREATH YOU GAVE
FOR THE MOMENT

CONTENTS

ACKNOWLEDGMENTS

I owe special gratitude to so many of the treasured souls who made
this book possible.

To my stalwart rock, Tom, and my certain gift, Alex, I'm so proud
of you both.

To Deb, my Joshua. It might have appeared to go unnoticed, but I've
got it all here in my heart! Thank you for loving me enough to
make me bleed. This project is all that it is because of you.

To my Peas and Carrots, thanks for chocolate milkshakes, prayers,
flowers, midnight phone calls, cards and more. You are my
nutrient providers: Bonnie Knopf, Lucy Kurz, Katy Vorce, Sandi
Shelton, Lorri Si, Dana Woolfolk, Myrene Morris, Yvonne
Polhemus, Claire Foster.

To J. D. Montei for a pure hug that led me to God!

To Jim Wilson, Hal Fetterman, Derek Packard, Bob Harrington, and
Mark Maddox, my business confidants and God's generals to me.

To my right hand, Deirdre. How could I live without your servant
smile, coffee, dry cleaning and more?

To Mike Terry, a real-life hero.

To my family, my mom, Patch, Kenny and Joe, your capacity for
strength amazes me. You're my inspiration to believe I could.

To my friend, Dave Clark; all right, already, I wrote it! Thank you.

I am eternally grateful to Wayne Hastings, who introduced me to
Eric Major, without whom this book may not have been
published. Thank you, Wayne, for your belief in me and my story
and for your strong encouragement.

ACKNOWLEDGMENTS

To Eric Major, who nearly convinced me God is English, and the Doubleday team. Thank you for embracing my life message.

To my pastors, J.R. and Yvonne, and all who believed in me.

To my grandparents, who gave me the gift of simplicity in a Bible, a quilt and southern love.

Thank you!

—Leisha Joseph

FOREWORD

All of my Bible heroes are survivors. I guess all of the people I have met in my life and consider to be my heroes are survivors.

This book is the story of a survivor. It is the story of a remarkable young woman who did not allow herself to be a victim but became a survivor. She did not look for social issues or society to blame but turned her violation and hurt into something positive, not only for her but for all of the people in her life. This is a story of God's love and grace, as well as a lesson of life. Pointing out that no matter how severe the hurt and pain, only God's love and grace allow us to triumph. It is the story of how knowing God and calling on Him actually saved someone's life in a time of grave danger.

Even though we are friends, the style of Leisha's book surprised me. First of all, it reads very well. Then it is so open and honest that you are hooked from the very beginning. I am glad she found a place to air such a delicate issue. There are probably many thousands of women who have experienced this trauma and are afraid to tell their stories.

When you first meet Leisha Joseph, you are touched by her beauty. Not her physical beauty but an inner spiritual beauty, the strength of her soul and character. She could have hidden this beauty with anger and resentment and a desire for revenge. Instead, she chose to open her spirit and soul to others. *Little Girl Lost* is her story's title, but the story of her life should be called "Little Girl Triumphant."

—Nicky Cruz

He lies in wait like a lion in cover;
he lies in wait to catch the helpless;
he catches the helpless and drags them off in his net.
His victims are crushed, they collapse; they fall under his
strength.
He says to himself, "God has forgotten; he covers his face and
never sees."
Arise, Lord! Lift up your hand, O God, Do not forget the
helpless.
Why does the wicked man revile God?
Why does he say to himself,
"He won't call me to account"?
But you, O God, do see trouble and grief;
you consider it to take it in hand.
The victim commits himself to you; you are the helper of the
fatherless.
Break the arm of the wicked and evil man;
call him to account for his wickedness
that would not be found out.
The Lord is King for ever and ever; the nations will perish from
his land.
You hear, O Lord, the desire of the afflicted;
you encourage them, and you listen to their cry,
defending the fatherless and the oppressed,
in order that man, who is of the earth, may terrify no more.

— PSALM 10:9–18 (NIV)

PROLOGUE

"The wicked man craves evil;
his neighbor gets no mercy from him."

— PROVERBS 21:10 (NIV)

He sat uneasily in the parked car, waiting and watching and trying to be inconspicuous. There are a number of reasons a man might be sitting all alone in a busy mall parking lot in the middle of a summer's day. He could be waiting for his girlfriend to buy a dress for their date that evening. He could be waiting to meet a buddy before they headed off to the ball game together. He could be a traveler who pulled off the road to look at a map.

But he was none of those.

The minute he saw her, he knew she was the one. She was tall, blond, and had a fresh, sweet expression. She looked so innocent. She got out of the car and seemed to float as she walked effortlessly, as if her feet didn't even meet the pavement. She was beautiful, but what gave him the most pleasure was her innocence.

She was the one.

He waited until no one was watching before he got out of his car and walked over to the car she had just left.

There are a number of normal reasons a man might pop the hood of a car in a busy mall parking lot in the middle of a summer's day. He could be tinkering with the engine as he waited for his mother to come out of the mall. He could be trying to diagnose a strange noise his car had just developed. He could be adding some oil to the engine.

But he was doing none of those.

The hood of her car easily creaked open and he reached beneath it and pulled the wires from the distributor cap. He slammed the hood shut. Making sure no one was watching, he slowly walked back to his car. He eased back into his car and slouched down in the seat. Beads of sweat pocked his forehead as he watched the ethereal heat waves shimmer upward from the steaming pavement.

And he waited.

Chapter 1

ECLIPSE OF THE SKY

*"The heavens declare the glory of God;
the skies proclaim the work of his hands."*

—PSALM 19:1 (NIV)

When I was small, my favorite place to hide was in a thick patch of grass that was taller and deeper green than the rest of my daddy's lawn. I used to bury my face in the tender blades and deeply breathe the sweet smell of summer. I'd pull up a long blade by the roots and chew the sweet white part, lie back and look at the sky.

From my vantage point, the sky stretched forever and beyond. Gigantic billowing clouds floated by like vast schooners sailing across a sea of blue. I wondered how high the sky reached beyond them.

From out of nowhere the thought came to me, I'll bet there's a God. There must be, look at all this.

I looked and pondered and gave God all the attention I could manage, which must have been about a minute and a half, before I jumped up and ran to the fort my brothers and I had built in the woods behind our house.

I didn't think about God too much when I was little, but that's really when my journey began. I knew Him the way most children do, through the love of affectionate parents and the acceptance and warmth that a close family can bring.

We lived in a large, rambling two-story house that Daddy had built with his own hands after a contractor had laid the foundation and frame. Towering oaks and leafy maples lined our street in an upper-middle-class neighborhood in the suburbs of Lambertville, Michigan. It was out in the country, really, in a tranquil farming community between Detroit and Toledo, Ohio. Our house was surrounded by large, sturdy trees for climbing, limber willows for swinging, ponds that froze over in the winter for ice-skating and the woods that my three brothers and I considered an annex to our rooms. We lived out there. Daddy had built our home in the middle of a kid's paradise.

He called me his princess, and I felt like one. For the very same mischief that would bring Daddy's wrath down upon one of my three brothers, I would get a smile, a wink and a mild reprimand. But my brothers didn't mind that much. Dad had taught them that boys were the protectors of the family, the big strong guys for whom he had different expectations. They were tough. They could take it. He was teaching them to take care of a family the way he did. But Mama and I were to be protected, cherished. We were special. Especially me.

My big brother's name was Roger, but everybody called him Patch. Daddy gave him that nickname when he was a baby because he slept in fits and starts, in little patches of time, not for hours like most babies. Patch, who was four years older than I was, teased me mercilessly and hid my dolls, but just let anyone else try to pick on me and he would rush to my defense.

My twin brother, Kenny, and I shared everything. He was my closest pal. Mama even dressed us alike. But we were crushed when we entered the second grade and were told we could no longer be together.

"You won't be in the same class this year," said the principal.

"But why?" I asked. "I like being with my brother and we always sit together and help each other."

"That's just it," she said. "We feel it will be better for you both if you don't help each other so much."

At that, Kenny was sent across the hall to Mrs. Kidman's class.

"Mrs. Kidman, the kid killer?" I frowned. That chubby, mean lady who wore ugly dresses, sensible shoes and had ankles like a tree? My chest sank and hurt so bad as I watched Kenny walk away to her class. We had always been together, it just wasn't fair! And who was going to watch out for Kenny and protect him? We were never allowed to be in another class again in all our schooling. At the start of each school year I would run to Kenny to check what class he was in.

"Separated again!" and I would spend the day crying inside. At night I would cry myself asleep wishing I could be with Kenny again. He was my best friend and they had no right to do this to us! From that point on, Kenny disliked school.

I'm not sure why, but I fought constantly with my younger brother, Joey, who was two years younger than Kenny and me. I recall the arguments usually centered around my Barbie dolls going on unauthorized dates with his G.I. Joe dolls when he wasn't around. He would come home and find a G.I. Joe keeping company with Barbie and he'd get mad and hit me. I would hit him back and we would become a tangle of thrashing arms and kicking legs until Mama pulled us apart. Daddy could break up a fight with one word and an intimidating look.

It seems to me now that Daddy's presence defined my days back then. He was the center around which my world revolved. When Daddy was in the house, we were all filled with feelings of comfort, safety and anticipation of fun. There was always so much laughter in my father's house. I loved to hear my dad laugh. The sound of it went straight to my heart. When he laughed, I knew we were safe, loved, and that all was well with our world.

Upstairs, where my three brothers shared two bedrooms, the laughter ricocheted off the walls while their footsteps pounded like thunder as each pushed the other out of the way in an attempt to be first down the stairs and at the table.

We gathered together at that table every morning for a big breakfast of eggs, bacon, toast and sausage that my mother had arisen early to prepare. I smelled the aroma of strong coffee that wafted from the kitchen, and struggled mightily to surface from the depths of my dream. Its grip was too tight. I surrendered to sleep once more only to be awakened by my mom's kiss a few minutes later.

"Wake up, sleepyhead," she said. "It's time for breakfast."

I jumped out of bed, raced to the bathroom to brush my teeth, then put on a dress that Daddy thought was pretty. I joined my brothers at the table, where we enjoyed Mama's wonderful cooking and good-natured teasing from Daddy. Moments later, Daddy was headed out the door to Continental Aviation Engineering, which produced aircraft engines for the government. Daddy was a supervisor for the testing chambers where the final tests on the engines were conducted.

I always ran to the door to give him a hug and kiss good-bye, then raced to my favorite spot on the couch in front of our big picture window that gave me a great view of our street. Mom had rearranged the entire living room and pushed the couch against the window to give me a comfortable place to sit as I watched Daddy's comings and goings. As usual, his car's bright lights flashed on and off, on and off, on and off, like swords that split the early morning darkness.

"Look at the headlights, Leisha," my mother said. "Daddy is blinking good-bye to you."

I waved frantically so Daddy could see me. Daddy eased the car out of the driveway, the headlights flashing on and off several more times. It was our very special good-bye.

I pressed my nose to the picture window and watched the taillights of Dad's car travel slowly down our street until I could see them no more.

"Time for school," my mother said as she ushered me away from the window and guided me to my bedroom to gather my things. "You don't want to miss the bus."

The aroma of fresh coffee lingered as my brothers and I struggled into our jackets and gathered our books for the short ride to Temperance Elementary, where my brothers and I attended school.

After school, I'd eat the snack Mama had for me, do my homework quickly, then snuggle into my favorite spot on the couch. My nose pushed hard against the big picture window, I watched the autumn leaves, delicate and red from the maple trees and buttery brown from the oak trees, twirl their way to the ground. Sometimes the wind would rise beneath them and send them soaring and spinning higher than the branch they had fallen from before they again swirled earthward and joined the piles already on our lawn. I watched the leaves and listened to the tinkling sounds from the kitchen as Mother made the final preparations for dinner, but my ears were straining to hear the comforting roar of my father's car bringing him home to us.

There it was! My heart leaped in my chest the second I recognized the sound and saw the familiar shape of Daddy's headlights separating the darkness.

"Where's my little princess?" Daddy would demand as he walked through the door, as if he couldn't see me running to meet him.

"Here I am!" I said, throwing my arms around his knees to hug the only part that I could reach.

He lifted me high off the ground and hugged me tight. I can touch the ceiling if I want to, I thought, but I never moved my arms from my daddy's neck. He set me down and was tackled by a tangle of boys who demanded that he wrestle and tousle them for a few minutes before we all joined Mama at the table.

My mother always set a beautiful table. Her stoneware dishes and glittering silverware were all in their proper places. In the middle of the table was a cornucopia full of miniature pumpkins, Indian corn and fruit. It was surrounded by platters piled high with home-cooked food. Mama was a wonderful cook.

We always had dinner together. Between bites of his dinner, Daddy nodded his head as we talked, and then he peppered us with questions about this teacher or that friend, or an upcoming ball game my older brother, Patch, would soon be playing. One night Mama interrupted the conversation.

"Please pass the salad dressing," she said to my daddy.

Perhaps he was prompted by all that sports talk, but Daddy picked up the salad dressing, paused for a second, then passed it as if he were the star quarterback heaving a football to a downfield receiver. The bottle of salad dressing landed on my mama's dinner plate with a resounding crack and shattered the beautiful stoneware.

Our laughter immediately dissolved into an astonished silence. How could this happen? What did it mean? Wide-eyed, we looked to my father to define the moment for us, searching his face for some kind of explanation.

Slowly his crooked smile broke loose across his face, saying it all. Mom had asked for a pass and she had gotten one. We exploded in laughter, my mom's the loudest of all.

My parents hosted parties for friends and family almost every weekend, and laughter rang through the rooms.

We would begin preparing for a weekend party early in the week, helping Mama with dusting and vacuuming. Even in the midst of all that mundane work, excitement and anticipation filled the air. Shortly after the bus dropped us off from school, our friends and family began to arrive all dressed up and carrying plates of food. But the party wouldn't really begin until Daddy came home from work. Everyone loved my jovial, funny daddy. He had so many friends.

We were always included in the parties. My brothers and I were each allowed our own bottle of soda pop, which we savored. Soda pop was a treat in our house, considered by my mama to be not very good for children, and so allowed only on special occasions. Carrying my precious soda, I would travel between the groups of congregating adults, sampling the conversations and stopping for a while when a good story was being told.

All too soon for my taste, it was time for bed. One last hug and kiss, and good-nights to all the aunts, uncles and friends, and Daddy shooed us off to our rooms.

"Off with you now," Daddy said. "Kids need their sleep."

"Awwww, Daddy, just a few more minutes," we would plead.

"Not one. Good night."

"Okay," I said as we obediently trotted off to our bedrooms. But the sounds of laughter and lively music always drew us like magnets to the stairway. We each claimed a stair, but in that walled stairway, we had to be happy just to listen to the fun, because we couldn't see anything. Eventually we tiptoed to the bottom of the stairs and peeked around the corner so we could watch the adults dance and laugh. I became bolder and slipped into the room to once more join the party, leaving my complaining brothers behind.

"Not fair!" Patch whispered loudly.

Maybe not, but I knew he wouldn't dare try to follow me. I turned around and gave him a sly grin.

Daddy was seated at the dining room table surrounded by a group of his friends. I slipped onto his lap. His face eased into that crooked grin.

"Who is Daddy's princess?" he asked.

"I am!" I exclaimed proudly, wrapping my arms around his neck and feeling successful.

"And what is Princess's bedtime?" he asked.

Uh-oh, here it comes. "Um . . . now," I said with a pout that was meant to melt his heart. I could see it wasn't working.

"Then let's get going. Princess needs her beauty sleep," he said, giving me another hug and kiss and sending me off with a playful swat on the behind.

Patch gave me a triumphant look from the stairs. He had won that round, but we both knew if he had tried that, the swat Daddy gave him wouldn't have been playful.

Our parties sometimes included my grandparents on my daddy's side, who were especially dear to us.

Grandma Jude, Daddy's mother, lived in Florida by the ocean, where Spanish moss hung gracefully from the trees and white sand slipped through our toes. She visited us often and sometimes we visited her. She was an excellent seamstress and taught me how to sew. At Grandma Jude's house, we could always wear shorts—that is, when she could get us out of our bathing suits.

My daddy's father was a Baptist preacher who had developed a drinking problem after he came home from World War II with an injury that kept him in constant pain. My grandparents had divorced as a result. Grandpa often came to stay with us, but Daddy had one rule: no drinking around us kids. If my daddy smelled liquor on Grandpa's breath, he made him leave. We always loved Grandpa's visits. He loved to cook and would make big pots of delicious soup that would fill the house with the most wonderful aromas of simmering chicken and fresh vegetables. He often pulled me up on his lap and read the Bible to me.

The autumn of my eighth year was long and lazy. Crisp golden days luxuriously unfolded before us, each seeming more beautiful than the day before as the deep green skyline yielded to blistering reds, bright yellows and oranges and toasty browns with the changing of Michigan's bountiful trees. Patch, Kenny, Joey and I helped Daddy rake our sprawling lawn, then tumbled in the piles of crunchy leaves, which sometimes meant we would have to do the job all over again. The weather was beautiful that year, and when there were no weekend parties, there were family outings to the movies or camping trips in the lush Michigan woods amid tall trees and sparkling lakes.

December arrived cold and blustery, but the gray sky had yielded no snow by the night of the fourth, when I pressed my nose against the picture window hoping to see large, lazy flakes drifting toward earth. My breath fogged the window. I squinted my eyes, and through the frosty glass the light from the streetlamps sprawled out on the pane and looked like giant stars.

"Come here, Princess, sit on Daddy's lap," my daddy said.

I left my spot at the window and snuggled up with Daddy in his favorite chair.

"What does Daddy's little princess want to watch on TV tonight?"

"Let's watch Billy Graham!" I said, remembering the television advertisement I'd seen earlier in the day that promoted the man who talked so lovingly about God.

"Billy Graham? Well, okay, Princess, whatever you want."

Daddy turned on the television set and we began to listen to the renowned evangelist tell the world that there was no better time than this to come to God.

"Boys, Elease, come and listen to this," Daddy said, calling us all together the way he did when something important happened, like when the astronauts first walked on the moon.

My brothers and our mama joined us in the living room. We sat quietly and listened as Billy Graham talked about God's love for each one of us. Daddy hugged me tightly and I looked up to see that his eyes were filled with tears.

The next morning, I hugged and kissed Daddy good-bye and heard the frozen ground crunch as he walked across our yard to the car. It was December 5, 1969. I didn't know it then, but it would be a day that I would never forget. I raced to my special place on the couch, jumping and landing knees-first, and waited for our special good-bye.

Daddy got in his car and slowly backed down the driveway. I watched and waited but Daddy's car kept going. He didn't stop! The headlights didn't blink! His car kept going all the way down the street. In confusion and feeling a little sad, I turned to Mama, who was standing behind me. It was the first time I ever remember that Daddy hadn't blinked our special good-bye.

Kenny said what I was thinking. "Daddy didn't say good-bye. How come, Mama?"

"Oh, honey, he probably forgot. He must have something on his mind. He hugged and kissed you good-bye, that's the important part. Let's get your coat on. It's time for school."

I pulled on my coat, thinking that I would have to remember to ask Daddy why he didn't blink good-bye when he came home from work.

After school, as the school bus headed down my street that frigid December day, I had forgotten that Daddy hadn't blinked good-bye to me that morning. I looked out the frosty bus window and wondered again when we would get our first snowfall. I thought how pretty the trees would look, all sparkly and glittery. But now they were dull and brown. I looked at the branches of the tall trees. Most of the leaves had already fallen, but a few brittle leaves, dead and curled up, still clung tenaciously to branches.

The school bus door swung open and I was surprised to see our driveway filled with cars. I hadn't known we were having a party! Oh boy, I thought, anticipating the fun we would soon be having.

"It's no party, Leisha," someone said.

Well, what is it, then? I wondered as I made my way down our stone driveway. Margaret and Dick Long, our next-door neighbors and our parents' best friends, met me and my brothers before we reached our house.

"You need to come to our house for a little while," Mrs. Long said softly, putting her arm around my shoulder and guiding me toward her house.

Mrs. Long's smile frightened me. Her mouth trembled a little and the rest of her face didn't smile along with her mouth. She looked sad, and like she was trying to hide it. I knew something was wrong, but no one would tell me what.

Mrs. Long sat us down with cookies and milk and then my brothers and I played board games with the Long children. Instead of our usual fun, anxiety and tension filled the house. Everyone seemed edgy. All Patch, Kenny, Joey and I wanted to do was go home to find out what was wrong, why everything was so unusual, why Mrs. Long wasn't her cheery self, why everyone looked at us so strangely.

Finally, after what seemed like hours, Mrs. Long gave us our coats and walked us next door to our house. The door swung open and my mind tumbled in confusion, trying to make sense of the scene. Our home was filled with all the familiar people, my uncles, aunts, neighbors and friends who always gathered at Daddy's parties, but no one was laughing and I could sense an oppressive dreariness. Everyone was so solemn and the sight of me and my three brothers caused some of them to wail loudly, and I was deeply frightened.

I made my way through the people looking for Daddy. He would explain all this. But I couldn't find his face in the sea of faces that surrounded me. Someone grabbed my hand and led me to the kitchen, where my brothers had already joined my mother.

Mama was seated on a chrome kitchen chair. Friends and family were all around her, embracing her as she held my hand and looked into my face. She looked so strange, her face anguished and puffy, and her hands were trembling. She looked much older than she had that morning. She opened her mouth to speak and could barely get the words out.

"Children," she said softly, but she was looking at me, "there's been an accident . . . Your daddy's dead."

I began to tremble. I don't remember crying, but Mama broke down before she could finish telling us what happened. I don't remember who supplied the rest of the words, but I began to realize there would be no party. There would never be another party.

Daddy had been testing a new turbine-powered engine and had entered the testing chamber to locate a technical problem. This powerful engine was so new that the safety devices had not yet been installed. They were sitting in boxes, lining the hallway outside the testing lab. No one had been aware of the mighty power this engine possessed. As Daddy approached the running engine, its tremendous force pulled him into the intake. The engine reversed, as it was built to do when obstructed, and Daddy's body was thrown with great force against the wall. Like a bird caught in a plane's engine, he never had a chance.

And now, at the age of thirty-seven, Daddy was . . . gone, someone told us. I wondered what he experienced. What went through his mind as he felt himself being sucked into the engine? Did he think of me? Did he know he was going to die? Did he feel pain?

In the days before his funeral our house was filled with people. People, people, always people and more people. They brought food and they cried. They brought flowers and they cried. They brought cards and they cried. They would take one look at me and cry. And there was planning and questions, and shopping trips for "proper" clothing, so much preparation.

"Your daddy is dead, Leisha, and you've got to accept it. That's what this funeral is all about," one concerned family member said to me as I sat in the funeral home, staring at my daddy in the casket.

All those faces that had been at our house that day I got off the school bus were there at the funeral, crying and sobbing. Grandpa's hands were shaking so, and Grandma Jude collapsed and had to be carried from the service.

Why did you have to leave me, Daddy? I thought as I watched people wail over his body. I could do nothing but stare and wonder. I felt so lonely at the funeral even though I was constantly surrounded by people, people who I knew loved me, but not one of them could take the place of my daddy.

This is a dream, I thought. Any minute now I'll wake up to the smell of coffee and Mama's kiss.

Strong men carried Daddy's casket to the big black hearse. Rain pelted the cars as we drove away from the funeral home on our way to the cemetery. It's fitting, I thought. God is crying with me. The sky was dreary, just like I felt inside, bleak and empty. The big black limousine pulled up in front of the gray stone building and Daddy's friends carried his casket inside. We were escorted to the front row of perfectly lined-up chairs. A shiver ran through my body and I couldn't help but tremble. This place is so cold, stone-cold and gray, just like my heart feels.

My big brother, Patch, lovingly put his arm around me, trying to comfort me and, I guess, trying to stop my trembling. For one second, I thought he was Daddy, then I felt a quick stab in my chest as I remembered why we were all there. Patch's loving embrace did more for me in that moment than he'll ever know. He had never done that before, we had been normal, battling siblings, and I had never seen him cry until then. A large tear ran down my cheek and I fully realized his place as the eldest son and the pain he must be feeling. My chest began to tighten and ache. I suppose that was the beginning of Patch trying to fill Daddy's shoes.

Close to my heart, I held secret fantasies that Daddy was still alive, long after the funeral, long after our house had emptied of people and had filled with a solemn hush. I envisioned an elaborate scheme that Daddy had faked his death because he was picked for a secret mission at work. I fantasized that he was really alive somewhere and had taken on another identity. Soon the mission would be accomplished and Daddy would come back home to me, I promised myself. I clung to my delusion until Christmas Eve.

Our house was dark and the chill of death still lingered there. Mama, my three brothers and I were invited to the Longs' house to try to celebrate Christmas. All of the other children seemed excited. Laugh-

ing, they shook some of the presents that were beneath the tree decorated with blinking lights and colored glass ornaments. The room
looked strange to me, as if a dark veil covered my face. My eyes couldn't
focus very well and the smell of fresh green beans cooking caused me to
gag.

I lay down on the couch and looked through the big picture window where sparkling snowflakes were softly drifting downward. The
excited voices of the other children sounded strangely muffled to my
ears as I lay there, dazed.

"I don't feel so well," I said. As I lifted my head from the couch, I
began to violently vomit. Mr. Long carried me to his car. Snowflakes
streaked past the windows like tiny shooting stars as he quickly drove
down the road. Some landed on the windshield and glittered for seconds before the swishing wiper blades cleared them away.

I was carried inside Dr. Clark's house. The sight of him and his
family around their dinner table, with the smell of fresh evergreen and
red and gold gifts beneath the tree, nauseated me.

It's not fair! I thought. Where is my daddy? I began to vomit again.

I awoke in a hospital bed.

"Shock," the doctor said. "She is in a state of shock from her
father's death."

I stayed in the hospital a week, my body and mind fighting to
overcome shock that I had been thrown into over my father's death.

One of my visitors was Reverend David Stephensen, a funny man
who often made me and my brothers laugh and who frequently went
hunting with Daddy. He used to say that Reverend Stephensen was a
"preacher man" who was always trying to get him "saved," whatever that
meant. He had been asked to give the eulogy at Daddy's funeral, but
didn't think he would be able to say the words without breaking down.

"God will give you the strength," his wife had told him, and so he
agreed and gave a beautiful and moving eulogy for my daddy.

When he arrived at the hospital to see me, I just knew he was a good friend of my daddy and me, so I welcomed the sight of him. But when he asked if he could pray for me, something inside me grew cold.

Why didn't you pray for my daddy? Why didn't you "save" him, I thought to myself as he was praying. I remember being angry when he left.

The next day, early in the morning, a new patient arrived. I peeked my head out of my door to watch as the nurses wheeled him down the hallway. What happened to his eye? I wondered. I just had to get a better look. After he was settled in his room, and the nurses had left, I tiptoed quietly down the hallway. I peeked through the cracked door and saw a lady standing over him adjusting his blankets. As she turned I caught a glimpse of her face. Mrs. Schragg! I thought, that's Mrs. Schragg, my second-grade teacher. What's she doing here, and why is she covering that boy? Now she's kissing his forehead! Just then I felt a firm hand.

"What are you doing out of your room?" the gruff nurse demanded, her hand resting solidly on my bony shoulder.

"Who is that boy?" I asked.

"That's Mrs. Schragg's son," the nurse said.

I had never thought of Mrs. Schragg as a mother and now the sight of her gently caressing her son, comforting him, caused something inside me to grow cold and lonely and I turned and walked down the hallway. I felt a great heavy weight pressing against my chest as I made my way to my room. There was an aching pain, a drawing inward. Something froze inside me right then . . . the fountain had been shut up . . . and it would be many years before I cried again.

Oh, I just want to go away and never come back. I just want this to be over. Without Daddy I will always be alone.

I came home from the hospital resolved that my life would be empty, this coldness would not go away and I would just have to learn to live with it.

Chapter 2

LITTLE
GIRL
LOST

*"I will search for the lost and bring back
the strays.
I will bind up the injured and strengthen
the weak . . ."*

— EZEKIEL 34:16 (NIV)

I came home from the hospital to a house as silent and solemn as a tomb. We were all so quiet, so numb, each of us deeply immersed in private mourning.

That next morning, instead of being awakened by the delicious aroma of fresh coffee, I was jolted awake by a shrieking teakettle where water boiled for Mama's instant coffee. The soft crackle of eggs in the cast-iron skillet that I was so accustomed to hearing the first thing in the morning was replaced by the constant flick of Mama's lighter as she readied herself with one cigarette after another, lighting a fresh one even before the first had been extinguished. As I watched my mama struggle with so much difficulty to pour simple bowls of cereal for us children, I ached for the energized mornings when fresh coffee perked and bacon smacked in the skillet as Mama prepared a full breakfast with ease, even as we children chased each other and threaded around her legs. I ached for my daddy's good-bye kiss, and for him to call me his little princess just one more time. I mournfully looked down at our black and white linoleum floor and brushed it softly with my toe. Daddy and I had installed that floor together one Saturday, tile by tile, side by side.

That evening the dinner table looked so empty. The stoneware was still in the cupboard; before us were paper plates. There wasn't much food on the table, and what was there didn't look very good to me. Daddy's chair at the head of the table was prominently empty. Everything seemed strange and Mama was not herself. She seemed sleepy and moved as if each time she picked up her arm or took a step, it required a great effort. She acted old, like Grandma, as if everything bothered her. No one ate very much.

As I looked at Daddy's empty place, I realized that laughter had left my father's house, and the resulting silence was deafening.

We missed our grandparents, but they, too, were struggling with their own grief and stayed away from us. My Aunt Mary Lou, Daddy's only sister, said it hurt Grandma Jude too much to see us just then.

We never got to see her again. Six months later, Grandma Jude died of cancer. She had been diagnosed with cancer six years earlier, and at that time the doctor had given her only months to live. After years rolled by with no symptoms, we thought she had beaten the disease. Aunt Mary Lou said Grandma just lost her will to live and had died of a broken heart. Our relatives kept her death a secret from us children until after the funeral, trying to spare us further suffering. But we were very hurt, and I was angry that I hadn't been able to see Grandma Jude one last time. As my uncles carried Grandma Jude's Singer sewing machine into our house, her final gift to me, I remembered sitting at her knee, learning how to carefully guide the fabric under the presser foot as she cautioned me to keep my fingers out of the way of the needle.

"That needle's not going anywhere but up and down, Leisha. Keep your eye on the fabric you're sewing and those sweet little fingers."

My precious, kind, laughing Grandma Jude, whose love enveloped us all like a warm embrace, was gone, too.

Grandpa began to drink heavily. Two months later, Grandpa died of cirrhosis of the liver. This time our relatives told us about his death and we were allowed to attend his funeral. I was so upset to see Grandpa in his coffin. As I looked at him, I was overcome with nausea from the overly sweet smell of carnations. I walked away from the visitation room and found an empty room, where I sat and stared at the wall. The funeral director looked in, saw me sitting there and put his arm around me.

"Are you okay?" he asked.

"I don't know why they have these things anyway," I said angrily.

"Why, honey, they have them for you," he said. "Funerals are not for the dead, they're for the living. This will help you accept that he is gone. If you don't accept it, you could be mighty troubled later."

He left me alone and I pondered what he had said. I was confused. Death had claimed my daddy, my Grandma Jude and my grandpa. I had accepted it, but that didn't give me much comfort. I was feeling mighty troubled right then and the pain of all the death and the loss was nearly too much.

It became common for my brothers and me to come home from school and find Mama lying on the couch fast asleep. She had never slept in the day before, but now she often did. I supposed it was the pills the doctor prescribed, "nerve pills," Mama called them. "Just something to help calm my nerves." But she began to take a lot of pills, it seemed to me. One was downed with her morning coffee, and one was taken in the evening after dinner. But soon she was asking us kids to remind her to take her pills in the day, too. She seemed to be continuously trying to wake up and she began to have frequent visits to the doctor.

"A psychiatrist," my brother Patch whispered to me.

We children tried our best to manage the house. I had always helped Mama dust and clean, but now I had to do most of it myself. I could manage dusting fairly well, but even when I leaned all my weight on the couch, I couldn't move it away from the wall to vacuum behind it.

Patch took over the laundry and Kenny voluntarily cut the grass—he loved to be outside. Joey wanted to watch cartoons, but Patch made him help me with the dishes. He was supposed to be rinsing and drying the dishes, but instead he put his hand in the rinse water and splashed me.

"Hey!"

He splashed me again.

"Cut it out!" I said.

He stopped only to twist the wet towel and snap it against my leg.

"Joey!" I yelled, and hit him hard with my fist.

Patch struggled up the stairs with a laundry basket piled high with clean blue jeans. "Stop it!" he ordered with all the authority of Dad. "There's work to be done around here. Get to it!"

Joey and I stopped our bickering and obeyed Patch as if he were our parent.

Although we tried our best to keep it clean, the house reeked of smoke. Ashtrays bearing mounds of stale cigarette butts littered each room. I am allergic to smoke and my lungs labored to breathe in that heavy, rancid air. We were all saved when Nina came to live with us. She was the mother of one of my daddy's close friends and became a paid companion for my mother, a substitute mother really, and a wonderful caretaker for my brothers and me.

Paid companions and private psychiatrists were not a financial hardship because, at the age of thirty-two, Mama had become a rich widow. Upon her husband's death, the house and two new cars had been paid off, and Mama was the beneficiary of a $300,000 life insurance policy that Daddy had increased by $100,000 just the year before. He had always taken such good care of his family.

Nina was older, grandmotherly, and had moved to Michigan from the Deep South. She spoke with such a pronounced accent, it was difficult to understand her at times, and often our friends made fun of her. But she was good to us. Throughout Mama's groggy days, it was Nina who made sure we got up for school in the morning, gave us breakfast, did the laundry and cooked dinner at night. With family nearby, Nina would sometimes leave us for a few days and visit with her own children, but she always came back to us. Mama seemed to sink deep within herself where none of our questions, or attempts at affection, could reach. Mama was there, at least we could see her body, but her mind and her spirit had drifted very far away from us.

We didn't realize how far she had gone until the day we stepped off the school bus and were startled by red flashing lights from police cars and an ambulance, all parked in our driveway. My brothers and I ran for the house and burst through the open door.

There was Mama, surrounded by big, strong men who were trying to force a straitjacket on her arms. She fought and kicked and screamed at them, her eyes as wild as a cornered tiger's.

Four powerful, strapping men were nearly not strong enough to subdue my petite mother, who must have weighed 120 pounds. With much difficulty, they grabbed her kicking legs and tied them together.

"What are you doing to my mother?" I began to scream at the sight. "Leave her alone! Stop! Stop!"

But they didn't stop. They were so involved with our mama, no one gave us one word of explanation. They lifted her from the couch and carried her through the front door, down the steps and into the awaiting ambulance, she screaming all the way.

I knelt on the sofa and, through our large picture window, watched in anguish as my only parent, clearly insane, was carried away. I hadn't believed it possible, but the gaping hole in my heart tore even wider as I began to realize that I had lost both my daddy and my mama. Suddenly the broad picture window at which I had beheld so many precious sights grew dark. Something that had been building up inside me was now ready to explode and I just wanted to hit that window right then, shatter it, send shards of glass flying into the horrific scene that was unfolding before me and make it go away. But I didn't. I froze. I choked back my emotions, shoved them down deep inside and locked them up until all I could feel was pressure building in my chest.

"Everything's gonna be all right, kids, I'm stayin' with y'all for a while," said Nina.

Nina was wonderful and we would have been lost without her. But . . . she wasn't Mama. I found myself living as a stranger in the house Daddy had built for us. Just as the window grew strange to me, so did the rest of the house. It didn't feel like home anymore, and the loneliness, the emptiness, grew deeper within me.

We don't know what Mama did that caused Nina to call for help that day. She wouldn't tell us. But Mama was taken away to a psychiatric ward in a private hospital, and it would be a long while before we would see her again.

Your mama has been good this week," Nina told us one afternoon, "and so ya'll can go visit her."

I was afraid to go, even though I desperately wanted to see her. My brothers and I walked, single file, down the hospital's long, cold, cavernous hallways behind an efficient, no-nonsense nurse. Her heels clicked on the polished, shiny floor and echoed in my ears.

My nose stung with the strong smells of medicines and disinfectants. People wearing surgical masks and scrubs seemed to close in on me as we followed the nurse to the "psych" unit, which was on the hospital's top floor.

We stood outside two sets of locked doors, and from the other side, we heard before we saw the nurse walk toward the doors, her many keys jingling from the chain at her waist. The sliding panel built into the door eased open and we saw eyes peering through at us, glancing side to side as if measuring us up. We heard the many locks unbolted, unlocked, unchained, one by one, and then we were face-to-face with eyes that peered from behind ancient horn-rimmed black glasses. The nurse was tall and dressed all in white. She was rather large, somewhat frumpy, with a forward brow and deep voice. Her clipboard and pencil in hand, she took our names and rattled off a list of rules and regulations that I thought would never end. We could only stay for a short amount of time and only in one particular area of the ward, and on and on and on. There were lots of rules and regulations. Her precise monotone lost me about halfway through. But when she came to the rule "No sharps allowed," I snapped to attention.

I didn't know then that the nurse was talking about anything pointed or sharp that patients could use to hurt themselves or others. At that tender age, I totally misunderstood. I had often been referred to as a "sharp" kid, and I thought she meant me. I kept my mouth shut so she wouldn't realize how sharp I was and make me leave.

The nurse led us to a game room of sorts and seated us at a round table. The room was dense with cigarette smoke, and other patients were there with their families. I lowered my head and, as subtly as possible, shifted my eyes and appraised the others in the room. An older woman was rocking back and forth in her chair and singing loudly and definitely off tune. Her visitors were ignoring her completely and playing a game of cards. At the next table was a young girl who looked about the age of my favorite cousin. She's probably a teen like Sandi, I thought, so what's wrong with her? She looks all right to me. Abruptly her sweet face changed and she began puffing a cigarette nonstop, one puff on top of another, so quickly I wondered how she could do that without choking. She stood up abruptly and screamed, "I hate you! I hate both of you!" then stomped out of the room. I guessed that the older man and woman who were sitting with her at the table were her parents. They glanced around the room quickly to see if anyone had been watching, then the woman's face began to crumble and large tears fell down her cheek. The man reached across the table and lovingly patted her hand.

Across the room, I heard a loud *clack!* Two men were playing a game of pool. Suddenly one of them heaved the pool stick over his head like a club and ran around the table toward the other man. A white blur went running past and two nurses grabbed the man, twisted his arms behind his back and guided him to the floor.

Amid this commotion, a nurse holding Mama's elbow led her gently to our table. She looked very different. Her hair was uncombed, she wore no makeup and she looked much older. I had always admired how Mama had always looked so pretty. She had always worn a bright red shade of lipstick to match her auburn hair and had worn colorful dresses or matched outfits. Always, just before Daddy was due to arrive home from work, she would comb her hair and make sure her lipstick was just so. But now her lips were pale, dulled and shriveled. She drew closer to me and grabbed me extra hard to give me a hug.

"Oh, I've missed you kids," she said, but her voice was trembling, and her hands! Her hands were shaking and they looked wrinkled and ugly. There were yellowish stains on her fingertips and nails. I soon realized those were nicotine stains as I watched Mama nervously light one cigarette after another.

"I need another carton of cigarettes and some shampoo," Mama said. "Can you have Nina send some up for me?"

"Mom, why do you have to stay here?" I asked.

"Mama is just sick, honey, but I'm gonna get better and come home soon."

But it was a very long time before she did come home, and at first, it was just for the weekends. On those weekend furloughs, we rarely saw much of Mama. She would make her way to the couch as soon as she arrived home on Friday and sleep for several hours. Then, as if magically transformed, she would awaken, not only revived but energized. She would spend hours getting ready to go out, carefully choosing a fancy dress and high heels. From a distance, I would watch her reflection in the mirror as she perfected her makeup and hair, and finished off with bright red lipstick.

"Why do you have to go out, Mama?" I would ask.

"Mom needs to keep her mind off things, honey, and dancing and being around people help me do that. You understand, don't you?"

"Sure, Mama, I understand," I said, replying as I was instructed. ("Leisha, don't you say anything that might upset your mother and try to be good so she won't get upset at all. Anything could set her off.")

But I didn't understand. Why couldn't Mama get her mind off things by being with us? Didn't we need to get our minds off of things, too? I thought. But mostly we needed her, we needed something she wouldn't or couldn't give. I felt betrayed, abandoned, unloved.

It wasn't until my adult years that I could see that Mama was trying to fill the vast void that had resulted from my daddy's death. Mama had loved and depended on him so very much. Her deep sense of loss was repressed, pushed down inside her, almost as deep as her hurt, and her body and mind reacted to the intense pressure by detaching from us, from life. Her sense of purpose and responsibility had become dulled, and she plunged into black depression. From her early years, she had suffered bouts of depression and Daddy had been her rock, her anchor in life, her protector, her compass. When Daddy died, Mama's connection to life had been too tenuous, too fragile, to sustain her. Daddy's death set off a reaction in Mama that would be out of control for many years.

I have only vague, distant memories of some of this, but family members have told me a chilling story that gives some insight into Mama's behavior about an event that occurred before my father's death. One day after Daddy had gone to work and Patch had gone to school, my mother became very depressed at the thought of being pregnant again. She wasn't pregnant, but became frightened that she could be again someday. My twin brother and I were young and at home and Joey was just a baby. I guess we were all too much for her. She sank deep into her thoughts and lost touch with reality. She reached for one of Daddy's guns from his collection, loaded it, placed it to her chest and squeezed the trigger. A loud noise rang throughout the house. I remember someone knocking at the door and that I ran to open it. It was the mailman who had been delivering our mail and heard the shot through an open window. He picked me up and sat me down on the couch, called an ambulance and saved Mama's life.

We children were sent to live with our Grandma Jude in Florida while Mama recuperated. I loved to run through the swinging screen door and hear it slam behind me as I ran down to the beach to play. There I could build huge sand castles and hunt for seashells and sit at the edge of the water and let it melt the sand between my toes. My brothers and I stuck together at the beach. Grandma said we should always stick together. One day Grandma let us take one of her metal cake pans down to the beach to play with.

"Wow, I can build a great castle with this, Grandma!" I said as we were leaving through the screen door.

"Just make sure you take very good care of it and don't let anyone else play with it," Grandma's voice echoed as we made our way to the beach.

We arrived to find a dark-haired girl sitting in our spot! My twin brother, Kenny, has never been the aggressive one, so I took the initiative.

"Hey, that's our spot!" I blurted out. "We were gonna build a castle there!"

"Well, why don't we build one together?" she suggested.

Why don't we build one together? I mimicked in my mind, but my ever-so-polite twin brother, Kenny, made his way over to concede. I thought I may as well go along, so together we began constructing our castle. We had the first level done and I could tell that this was going to be the best castle yet. My thoughts were interrupted when the girl with long dark hair lifted my grandma's pan and banged it on a rock to loosen the damp sand that had become stuck in it, and caused a large dent on the bottom.

"You dented my grandma's pan," I heard Kenny say.

"So what!" she retorted.

Meek Kenny said, "My grandma said to take care of it."

"So what do you want to make of it?" she said, sticking her nose right in Kenny's face.

I was enraged! She wasn't going to push my brother around like that, or get away with bending my grandma's pan. I jumped up from the sand and headed for her. Kenny backed off when he saw me coming full speed. I lunged at her and grabbed Grandma's pan from her grip. She toppled backward and landed right in the water. I grabbed Kenny's hand and ran up the sand dune toward Grandma's. When we told Grandma what happened she laughed so hard, her plump belly bounced up and down. She grabbed us both and gave us a big hug and told me to always watch out for my brothers, especially Kenny.

I think that was the beginning of our bond of sticking together. Somehow we knew we just had to. Mama recovered and we left Grandma's for home. I felt all mixed up the day we left. I liked Florida. I especially liked the train conductor. Every day at the same time a train came down the tracks that were near the house. The conductor would blow his whistle and all the children would come running. He'd pull the train to a dead stop and begin to fling Hershey's kisses out of his window. I firmly believed chocolate is God's food for the soul. We scurried to catch the flying candy, and the sound of the whistle blowing made it a wondrous affair.

I always wondered why Daddy cried the day we came home. He was never one to cry, especially in front of us kids. I thought then that he was just happy to see us. But I realized later how deeply hurt he must have been when my baby brother, Joey, did not recognize him. In fact, he was afraid of Daddy and wouldn't go to him for a long time. But time passed and Joey warmed up to Daddy, and Mama became well. Other than those dim recollections of opening the door to the mailman, I don't remember anything of Mama's early depression. And so as a child I had no perspective, no understanding of what Mama was going through after Daddy died. I just remember that I wanted desperately for us to be a family, some kind of family. I remember trying to get close to Mama, to be included in her life, only to have her shoo us away as she headed out the door to make the rounds of the clubs and bars.

Nina was there with us, of course, but it seemed so unsettled when Mama should have been home with us and wasn't. It was so different from the way we lived when Daddy was alive, I had a difficult time adjusting to what our family had become.

We children became a unified front, pulling together, I guess, in an attempt to provide some type of stability. As time went on, Patch took on more and more adult roles, growing up long before his time. The exceptions were Joey and I, who continued our battles until the day he hit me in the stomach, hard, and I doubled over in pain. I was having a difficult time crying because he had knocked the breath out of me. I stood there, bent over and gasping, and Joey's eyes widened in fear.

"I'm sorry," Joey said. "I really hurt you. I don't know why I hit you so hard."

That was the last time Joey ever hit me back. Sometimes I took my rage out on Joey. I would hammer his back, his arms, and all he ever did was cover his face with his hands. He never hit me again.

One night when I was ten, Mama arrived home very late from the bar. I know it was late because I had lain there for hours waiting to hear her come in. I pulled up my covers and shut my eyes as if sleeping, just in case Mama peeked in on me. My bedroom was right across the hall from Mama's and Daddy's. Daddy always said he wanted his little princess close by at night so he could be sure I was safe. How I wish he had been there this night! I could hear Mama laughing. Why would she be laughing to herself? I thought to myself, Oh, I hope she's all right. Then I heard another voice, a deep voice, a man's. Who could that be?

Why would someone be visiting this late? I tiptoed out of bed and peeked down the hall. My innocent thoughts deteriorated as I saw a man kissing my mama.

"You're drunk!" I could hear Mama say. "Here, you sleep it off here on the couch." Mama covered him up and I hurried back to bed as Mama headed toward her bedroom. I tried so hard to fall asleep while struggling to understand why Mama would kiss someone other than Daddy. A deep hurt lodged in my chest, but I had learned how to make that hurt go away. I froze all my emotions, shut them down. I would not allow myself to feel anything. I would not cry, my jaw clamped down and locked in distress.

I finally drifted off to sleep, my fists still clenched and my jaw locked. I was awakened by a figure standing over me. The outside light that streamed through my window outlined the figure of a man. By the stench of alcohol, I realized it was the man Mama had covered on the couch. As he approached I squinted my eyes shut tightly, pretending to be fast asleep. What does he want? Maybe he's looking for the bathroom. Maybe I should show him . . . maybe I'd better just pretend I'm asleep and not make waves. I became very good at pretending I was asleep. He made his way toward my bed and lay on top of me, mumbling something through his liquor breath. He moved around all over me and placed his rough hands on me. I kept my eyes shut in horror as he tried to kiss me. I rolled over as if still asleep, hoping he would leave. I thought his weight would crush me.

Just as suddenly as the nightmare had begun, it was over. I opened one eye slowly and he was gone. I lay there, frozen in fear, not even twitching one muscle. I didn't return to sleep that night, nor for many nights to come. The morning arrived and I lay there still frozen. What should I do? I thought. Should I get up? Did I dream last night? I was afraid to move. I began to sweat under the covers that I had pulled tightly under my chin.

"Leisha! Leisha, it's time to get up!" I could hear Nina's voice echoing down the hallway. Slowly, placing one toe at a time to the floor, I managed to make my way to my closet. Surveying my clothes hanging there, I froze in a stupor.

"Leisha, are you all right? Do you feel okay?" Nina stood in the doorway to my room. "Hurry up, your breakfast will get cold."

I hurriedly dressed and made my way down the hall. There was no one on the couch! Where was he? Did I dream all that? Maybe I'm going crazy like Mama, I remember thinking. I went to school and spent that day in a daze. I could hear no one. I felt strangely disconnected, but I was functioning, so I knew I wasn't dreaming.

Mother never drank much, but in the smoke-filled bars she found something in the companionship of those she met that eased her pain. Mama had a string of boyfriends who disappeared from our lives just as quickly and mysteriously as they arrived. Included among them was the man who had come into my room that night. To my great relief, he never came back. No one stuck around very long until Mama met Bill. Not long after they met, Mama called us together and told us she had met someone special and would be married within a few months. Even though he was a friendly-faced man who seemed to genuinely like us, my heart sank at the announcement. I knew I was supposed to be happy for her, but the ache for Daddy was still there. How could she do this to Daddy? I thought. She doesn't even care. How could she do this to us?

Mother and Bill were married and we gained two stepbrothers and a stepsister and lost Nina. The children lived with their real mother and we only saw them on weekends when they came to stay with their father. I liked my stepsister, Shelly. She was nice, and though a bit older, she always talked with me. We had some fun times. Once, we vacationed together as a family in Maryland and stayed with Bill's sister, who lived near the ocean. It reminded me of my grandma's house. We had a fun time of burying each other in the sand, hunting for crabs and fishing in the boat. Even though I was surrounded by my mama, three brothers, a stepfather, stepsister and two stepbrothers, there was an underlying loneliness in my heart that wouldn't go away.

When we got back home, Mama became ill again and this time she was even worse. Between the long drive to and from the mental hospital, and the full responsibility for us kids, Bill decided it was all too much. Soon Bill and my mama were divorced and my Uncle Mitch and my Aunt Mary, who was my grandpa's sister, came to live with us.

Uncle Mitch was a kind old man who had lost a leg through diabetes and couldn't get around very well. He would often sit out in the yard and whittle or carve on a piece of wood to pass the time, and he was always ready to share a story. I found great solace in sitting on his knee listening to stories, some about Daddy. Aunt Mary was kind to us, too. Though outspoken (she often scared my friends with her loudness), she did her best to keep up with us kids.

We had come to accept as normal Mama's cycle of mental hospitals, where doctors tried to medicate her, and the bars, where she tried to medicate herself. She had been receiving shock treatments from the first hospitalization. Doctors had hoped that the electricity that shot through her brain like a lightning bolt would stimulate some kind of recovery. But all the treatments did was rob her of many precious memories. Then doctors pumped her full of heavy psychotropic drugs such as Haldol and Thorazine in an attempt to control her erratic behavior. They bestowed impressive diagnoses upon her, such as paranoid schizophrenic. When she came home she would always seem to be better for a while. Then she would decide she didn't need the medication anymore because it made her too sleepy and stole her energy. So she would stop taking her pills and it would not be long before she turned into someone we didn't know. She would get better and then worse and then better again and then worse than ever. It was a vicious cycle that would continue throughout my growing-up years as I literally watched my mama deteriorate before my eyes.

There were Christmases when we children helped Mama ever so carefully place tinsel and angel hair, her favorite decorations, on a tall evergreen whose spreading branches filled an impressive section of the living room. Afterward, the zesty smell of fresh pine would fill the house and powdered sugar would fall on the floor like snow as we all gathered in the kitchen to decorate heaping plates of delicious sugar cookies that Mama had spent hours baking. And then there were Christmases when the only decorated trees we saw were in store displays and when Mama's oven was as cold and dark as a cave. There were times when Mama told us we were wonderful, talented and precious to her and that we could be anything in the world we set our hearts to be. And there were times when she lay on the couch in a Haldol-induced stupor and waved us away as we tried to tell her about an A we'd received on a spelling test. The worst for me was never knowing what to expect. Would I come home to Mama? Or would I come home to a stranger who ranted and raved about murder conspiracies formed against her by store clerks and mailmen? Would I come home to a frenzied wild woman with hair like dead weeds and the strength of a man, who flew at me with flailing arms and eyes afire? I never knew, as I opened the front door, who or what would be there to meet me.

And I never knew when another of the boyfriends she brought home after the bars had closed would make their way into my room, reeking with liquor and stale sweat, put their hand over my mouth and press down upon me as they already had done more times than I cared to remember.

I tried to escape in my art, which, even at that early age, was very important to me. I would take great care drawing the most beautiful house I could think up with the most luxurious landscaping I could picture and then I would imagine myself living inside that crayon drawing, surrounded by normal, loving parents and happy brothers.

Uncle Mitch became increasingly ill with diabetes, and during one of Mama's many "recoveries," he and Aunt Mary went back to their own home, which was about thirty minutes away from our house. Churchgoing neighbors used to visit my mama regularly and pray with her. But Mama made it difficult for anyone to help her or us. I often overheard her arguing with Daddy's friends, our neighbors and family, rejecting any offer they made, in a kind of prideful arrogance.

"I can take care of my kids!" she'd scream at them. "I don't need your help. I don't want anyone's charity."

They would always leave. I was hesitant to invite anyone over to my house to play. I didn't know if Mama would come out of her room half-dressed or screaming obscenities, always with a cigarette hanging out of her mouth.

"Put a robe on, Mama, please," I would plead.

"I'm hot," she would say. "And besides, I don't dress to please other people. I don't care what anyone thinks."

She would talk and talk and talk about absolutely nothing at all—at least none of it made any sense to me. She would go from one subject to another without pause. And she was very smart; she had a fine, intelligent mind and knew a lot about many things. She wove in legitimate facts with her nonsense and so it took several minutes before it was apparent that the conversation was absurd.

When she was Mama, she was sensitive, caring and loving. But there were times you would swear she housed demons in her heart. She would never intentionally torment us, but we lived in an environment that was tormenting.

We walked on eggshells trying not to set her off, and we never knew what the trigger would be. It was always different, it never made any sense to us. Instinctively we children developed a secret code, a way to communicate without opening our mouths. Patch would come in the door, and my eyes, my body language, would tell him to be careful, that Mama was on the verge of "being set off" again.

She became obsessed with Daddy's death. She talked endlessly about how we all should have known when he didn't blink his headlights that morning that he was going to die. And didn't he watch Billy Graham with tears in his eyes the night before? They were omens, signs, and we didn't notice.

"We could have stopped it!" she ranted at us.

When we were younger, we were traumatized by this possibility. We wrung our hands, wailed together and felt guilty, although we didn't quite understand why. As we grew older, we sighed and tried to tune her out.

A neighbor who worked in the grocery store was a first-rate gossip and soon the story of Mama's flight from sanity was all over town. It wasn't long before I had no friends; their parents wouldn't let them come to our house.

"My mom says I can't come over to your house anymore," Peggy told me. "She said your mother is crazy."

I heard that more than once. Those words cut me in two. I began to grow despondent with the shame, the awful shame that a deep-seated terror had come true: everyone knows! Everyone in the entire neighborhood knows that Mama is crazy. Contempt and rage began to build in me. It was my only defense to diminish the intense humiliation of being exposed. But there was one person who remained a friend, Jackie.

Jackie was skinny and blond, like me. Her family lived next door and Jackie and I spent a lot of our time in the sand pile next to our house or off playing in the woods.

"I've got to go, Leisha, I've got to get home in time for church," Jackie often said.

"You're always going to church," I said.

"Why don't you see if you can come with me?" she always replied.

"I don't think I can," I'd say, thinking to myself, what would I do at a church? It was such a foreign idea to me and I felt sorry for Jackie that she had to go so much. I thought it was bad enough having to go to school every day, let alone church to hear some hypocrite preacher spout off about "saving" somebody. Nobody had saved my daddy.

Every time her family went to church, which was three times a week, Jackie invited me to go with them. I made up every excuse I could think of not to go. I just couldn't see myself in church. It sounded like such a boring idea and I remembered how Reverend Stephensen had angered me. Somehow I felt he could have prayed my daddy back, but didn't.

"Why don't you come to church with me, Leisha?" Jackie asked me one day for the countless time.

I hesitated. Jackie was my friend, my only friend, in fact, and I didn't want to lose her, too. "Well, okay," I said reluctantly. "But just this once."

I stood in front of my closet, stumped. What in the world was I supposed to wear? I fumbled through my clothes. No one had shopped for me in a very long time. All my pretty dresses, the ones Daddy had loved, were many sizes too small. All I had were hand-me-downs from my brothers, blue jeans and flannel shirts, mostly. I know! I'll wear one of Mama's dresses! Mama had so many pretty dresses with shoes dyed to match. Sometimes when she was away at the hospital I'd slip into her room and go through her closet. She had a large jewelry box full of costume jewelry. I loved to pretend I was all grown-up, going out for the evening, and the only trouble on my mind was what to wear. I made my way to Mama's closet. Most of the dresses were on their hangers. Mama had taken mostly pants to the hospital this time. I found one I thought would fit and snuck it into my room. I zipped it up and ran to the mirror expecting to see a smaller version of Mama. But I was so disappointed with the vision before me. The dress fit everywhere but at the top, which was sagging down to my waist. I was only twelve and puberty wasn't even in my vocabulary yet.

I wound up wearing my blue jeans to Jackie's house. I arrived early and nervously knocked on her door. I always got nervous when I went to someone else's house. I always had a sense that everyone else lived "normally," not like I lived. I was petrified I might find myself in a situation where I wouldn't know how to act. Jackie's mom answered the door. She was a pretty lady, tall, elegant and always composed.

"Leisha! Welcome and come in. I'm just finishing my hair and then we'll be ready to go. Have a seat."

I sat down and watched her brush her beautiful blond hair. How can she always look so pretty? I thought.

Jackie came into the room. She had pants on! What a relief. We got in the car and Jackie's mom sang something very pretty all the way to church. We got to the church early, but there were lots of people already there. I was amazed and a little shocked to see people hugging each other. What is going on? Maybe somebody died, I thought. I hadn't really seen anyone hug like that, nor had I been hugged in a pure way, since Daddy died, four years ago. We walked down the aisle on a deep red carpet. The pews were thick, real wood and there were dainty, delicate flowers lining the altar. Jackie's mom left for a while and we sat down in the pew together. Immense stained-glass windows lined each sidewall and I gazed intently at them in wonderment as the evening sun set behind them, sending rainbows of color dancing around the room.

There was a warm feeling here that I couldn't explain, something I hadn't felt in a long time. Soon, Jackie's mom returned and she had someone with her. A tall lean man, like Daddy.

"Leisha, this is Pastor J. D. Montei," she said.

I stood up and before I knew it he had reached his arms around me and was hugging me. "Leisha, I'm just so glad you're here with us today," he said, sounding so genuine.

"Uh . . . thank you," I said, pulling away from him.

The service was about to begin and he left to make his way to the platform. As I sat there in the pew, something inside me was beginning to melt. I think he really meant that! I thought. I remember when Daddy used to hug me like that, it felt so safe, so warm.

The music began and it was nothing like I'd expected. I had been to vacation Bible school at the Methodist Church with Jackie when we were younger and we always sang out of books, but here there was a lady up at the platform putting overheads with the songs on them on a screen. Then the musicians began to play. Hey, a drummer and a guitar! That's pretty cool! Soon the music started and everyone around me was clapping their hands to the beat. My eyes widened and I wondered what I was supposed to do. I watched Jackie and imitated everything she did.

Pastor Montei got up and began to talk. It was real nice. Everything he said seemed to make sense. Then he said, "Someone sitting in church wants to commit, but is holding tight to the pew, so tight their knuckles are turning white."

He must be able to see me from way up there! I thought.

"I would ask you to come, just now, just as you are. Make your way to this altar and God will meet you and embrace you in His loving arms like a father . . ."

In the background, "Just As I Am" was playing softly and the singers began to sing. Hey! I thought, that's just like the Billy Graham show I watched with Daddy!

I sat back and watched to see what would happen as several people made their way down to the front. The music kept playing and the preacher kept calling.

"God will embrace you like a father" kept echoing in my ears. "God will embrace you like a father . . . God will embrace you like a father."

Something hot began to trickle down my cheek. I was surprised to see a tear fall on top of my now bone-white knuckles that clutched the pew. As I looked up, another tear fell and the music changed. "It's for those tears I died. I felt every teardrop when in darkness you cried and I strove to remind you that it's for those tears I died."

"God will embrace you like a father . . ."

I found myself walking down the aisle, making my way down to that altar, shaking violently from a deep vibration that pounded from within and crying for the first time in four years. I fell on my knees in front of the pastor and wept and wept and wept. I couldn't stop weeping and it felt so good, so clean, so warm.

Then Pastor J.D. put his arms around me and just held me like Daddy used to and I felt so warm, so loved, so safe once more. Pastor J.D. hugged me with all the love of Jesus and something inside me melted. I felt the genuine love of God and invited Him into my heart. I knew He was real and that He cared.

Pastor Montei became like a daddy to me. He always had a hug for me when I came to church, which was very often. Jackie's parents picked me up for church every Sunday, every Wednesday and every Friday for youth group. I loved going. I got to be with Jackie and out of my house. It felt good to be in a place where you knew what to expect. At home, at least when Mama was home, I had to be on guard constantly.

One Friday I came home from school to find Mama, sitting at the table in our family room and sipping instant coffee between drags on her cigarette. We hadn't expected her home from the mental hospital until the next day.

"Mama, you're home early," I said as I reached to put my arms around her neck to hug her.

As I touched her, she flung her arm up and knocked my arm away! I stood there stunned as she let out a grumbling noise. A fierce terror came over me as her face began to twitch, contort and twist into someone who didn't even resemble my mama. She opened her mouth and out came ugly groaning noises, directed at me. I backed away. She picked up the book of matches lying on the table and began to strike one after another, throwing each lit match onto the carpeted floor. I hurried over to her and ground out each match as it landed on the singed carpet.

"I'm gonna burn you down!" she grumbled, almost in a man's deep voice. "I'm gonna burn this house down! I'm going to burn you down. You don't care about me! You want to kill me! You all want to kill me!"

"But, Mama, that's not true!" I cried out. "Please don't do this!"

"*Get out!* You get out of here before I burn you down to nothing!"

My mind snagged on a deep, distant memory. Before Daddy had built our lovely home for us, there had been another home where it stood. It was a modest bungalow with just enough bedrooms for all of us. I can still see the matching checked bedspreads in the room my twin brother, Kenny, and I shared. I began to remember our checked bedspreads lying in the rubble, burned! Our house had burned to the ground one day while we were at school. Daddy was at work and Mama was working as a manager in a department store. It was horrible to see all our things burned and melted, and the smell was awful! I watched Daddy's face convulse as the bulldozer pushed what had been our beds, clothes and toys into piles of twisted and melted rubble.

"We don't know what caused the fire, sir," the firefighter said. "We just thank God none of you was home."

And here was Mama throwing matches onto a carpet that could ignite at any minute in the beautiful new home that Daddy had worked so hard to build back for us.

"Mama! You don't know what you're saying!" I said as I grabbed her by her wrists to stop her.

But her strength was incredible. With the power of ten she easily pushed me to the floor. I crawled away from her and ran to get my big brother. Patch realized Mama was very sick. He called an ambulance and I watched them take my mama away again, screaming, fighting, kicking. This time would be different, however. Mama had to be committed to the state mental hospital, a requirement of state law, because she was clearly dangerous to herself and others. And Patch, at the tender age of sixteen, would have to be the one to testify to that fact in court. Patch felt a great burden to be the head of the family. What a heavy responsibility he carried so young. Patch was a lot like my daddy, strong, stable and seemingly unshakable despite the emotional earth-quakes going on around us constantly. There were so many times he protected us and held us together. I know he went through great an-guish and torment at having to take the stand and tell the judge the awful things Mama had been doing. For the first time, Mama wasn't at a gentle, private hospital where she could check herself in and check herself out on the weekends for parties. This time, Mama was being held against her will in a locked unit with other dangerous people, and she was furious.

The day Patch had to testify, I watched him get ready to go. As he adjusted his tie in the large mirror that hung in the living room, I could see the despair in his eyes. My big brother who teased me, hid my dolls and tickled me until I turned blue was now a man in a suit and tie with heavy lines around his eyes. Something inside me welled with hurt as I felt the heaviness of what he would face that day.

"I want to go, Patch," I said.

"Leisha, you can't. Besides, there's no use of it. You don't need to see Mom like she is."

I grabbed his neck and hugged it tightly. It was the beginning of Patch bearing the heavy load of caring for us children, the household, and keeping the family together. The judge committed Mama to the state mental hospital and she became angry and embittered toward Patch. She blamed him for everything, for all the hurts and wrongs that had ever happened in her life, for her inability to function, for her being locked up in a hospital full of menacing souls much like herself, for her shattered life. She told him she hated him for what he had done to her and that she would never forgive him.

Chapter 3

A SAVING GRACE

"But because of his great love for us, God,
who is rich in mercy, made us alive with
Christ even when we were dead in
transgressions—it is by grace you have
been saved."

— EPHESIANS 2 : 4 – 5 (NIV)

M y brothers and I had become accustomed to the strange behavior we had seen at the psychiatric wards when we visited Mama, but nothing had prepared us for what awaited at the state mental hospital, which was crowded with chronically mentally ill people.

It seemed to us that Mama was getting worse. Sometimes she would ask me to read the Bible to her, and she seemed to find comfort in the words. After visits, I would go to church and pray for God to make her better. But the more I prayed, the worse things became until the day we were all waiting for Mama to be escorted to us and a strong hand gripped my shoulder. I looked up into the haggard, sneering face of a large woman who howled at me and dug her fingers deeper into my arms. Her screech was primitive and guttural. It shot chills up my back. I pushed at her, and a male nurse raced over to the table, pried her hands from my arms and led her away. An older woman with stringy, gray hair took her place and began swaying back and forth, scowling at me.

"You think you're so pretty, don't you?" she hissed in a raspy, hoarse voice. Several patients joined her, slowly walking toward me like zombies, swaying from side to side and loudly chanting a jumble of odd words that I couldn't understand. One of them grabbed my shirt and tried to rip it while another began stroking my arm. My brothers were stunned. Before they could react, a nurse pushed her way through the crowd of patients and took me into a room.

"That's it!" she shouted. "I have orders from the doctor for you."

"What do you mean?" I asked, confused.

"Every time you come up to this hospital we have a whole slew of patients to deal with when you leave. You cause certain patients, including your mother, to become religiously preoccupied. We have even had to seclude some patients after you've been here."

"What are you talking about?" I asked.

"I'm sorry, but you will not be allowed to visit your mother again and please put away that Bible!"

They let me spend a few minutes with Mama before they made me leave. She asked me to read the Bible to her, but I read only one Scripture before I left. On the ride home, I kept trying to understand. What in the world is "religiously preoccupied"?

That incident marked the beginning of a war between myself and Mama and her professionals. Suddenly I, a young girl, was no good for Mother and was to blame for some of her problems. I asked God to help me understand.

With Mama away again, we were once more living by ourselves, with Patch working at a factory to support us. One day I answered a knock at the door to greet our aunt and uncle and the police.

"We want to ask you a few questions," the police officer said to Patch.

"What's all this about?" Patch asked.

"Now, Patch," I heard my aunt say, "we are all worried about you kids, we just want to make sure you're all taken care of. We only want what's best."

"Leisha! Go in the other room," Patch ordered. "Right now!"

I left, but I could still hear them talking. My aunt and uncle wanted to split us children up and place us with relatives, and the police were there to help them. But Patch refused to allow it.

"You can't do this," Patch said. "I am taking care of these children. I am working, I'm buying food and clothes for them. Go check in the kitchen and you'll see there's plenty of food. You have no right to take them."

They talked for a long while and eventually my aunt, uncle and the police left.

"We're gonna stick together, kids, we're gonna make it!" Patch told us after they left, and many times afterward, and we were strengthened by his sheer belief in us.

I threw myself into church and school activities. Art, which had always interested me, became my sanctuary in school. Wrestling was a major sport in my town and girls could become involved through the Grapplerettes, the wrestling cheerleading squad. The squad kept track of scores and records, painted posters that were displayed on game day and cheered the wrestlers on from the stands. Girls had to study wrestling fundamentals and pass a test before they were seriously considered. While I had a strong desire to compete in sports, I was rather frail and never did well, and so I tried out for the Grapplerettes, and made it.

Church continued to be important. I never missed Friday night youth group. Mrs. Tanis always met us with brownies and a big hug at the door of her large, warm home, where we met. Our youth leader played the guitar and we always gathered in a circle to sing praise songs after the Bible lesson. I never felt I completely fitted in because everyone else's parents were involved in the church, but I so enjoyed those Friday nights.

The youth group often took trips, and it was during the weeklong Jesus festival in Pennsylvania that I heard the words that would change my life. Many famous preachers spoke, but no one stirred my heart like country preacher David Wilkerson, who told us about venturing into New York City's violent streets to tell teenage hoodlums that God's endless love extended to them, too. He told teenagers who had killed, stolen, raped, and who were addicted to heroin that they could be forgiven for all the sins they had committed against God and humanity, that they could be redeemed through Jesus Christ. He told them that God loved them no matter where they had come from, and if they didn't have a family, God would give them the family of God.

One young gang leader would hear none of it. Nicky Cruz put a knife to Wilkerson's throat and threatened: "Shut up, preacher, or I'll kill you."

But Wilkerson was calm and confident in God. His loving response burned itself into my mind: "Go ahead," he said. "Even if you cut me into a thousand pieces, every piece will continue to love you."

Those words stopped Cruz cold, and eventually Cruz, a homeless boy who had been abandoned by everyone, including his own family, became one of Wilkerson's strongest converts.

I found in Cruz a kind of kindred spirit, and I marveled at the strength and courage of David Wilkerson to be able to deliver such a gentle response in the face of death. What guts, I thought. What power! If only I could have such undaunted faith. And I began to pray to become that strong in God someday.

My understanding of God was beginning to grow. It was during this time of spiritual encouragement that I went to a youth meeting with my friend Jackie to find a lot of whispering. Many of the regular kids were missing, and even our teacher seemed distraught. And where was Pastor Montei?

Soon everyone was talking about the church split, which is a disagreement over some issue that divides the church right down the middle. Pastor Montei was replaced and people whom I'd grown to trust were saying awful things about the man who had taught me about God's unfailing love. I never learned the full story, I was just a kid on the sidelines. I couldn't understand how my pastor, the man who baptized me and hugged me each week and encouraged me like a father, could suddenly be all those names they called him.

Jackie's parents stopped attending that church and invited me to go with them to a different one, but I never felt at home there. After visiting a few times, I stopped going. I had no way to get to my old church, and slowly the familiar cold heaviness and the certainty that I would always be alone again began to suffocate my heart. Once more, all that I had put my hope in was gone. I was terribly wounded. I tried to make sense of it and couldn't. I concluded they were all hypocrites and that no one had meant a word they had said. All that church stuff, what a lot of baloney. Maybe the nurse and Mama's doctor were right, maybe I was "religiously preoccupied." Deep in my spirit, I resolved not to love anyone or anything ever again. The loss of love hurt too much.

I was entering junior high school and my life was becoming complicated. The first few weeks of school were a nightmare. It seemed as if everyone but me was wearing makeup and had pretty, new dresses. All I had were flannel shirts and jeans, my brother's hand-me-downs. I felt like an outcast. I tried to fit in, but I barely knew how to comb my hair, let alone what to say to these kids, and so I kept to myself. I ate lunch alone, avoided crowds of laughing kids and kept my head down so no one would notice me. I tried to blend in with the walls and the furniture.

Shortly after school began, a new girl moved into our neighborhood. She was pretty, wore beautiful clothes and was popular with boys. And she was nice, even talking to me on the bus. From a safe distance, I often watched her talking and joking with the other kids. I tried to figure out exactly what it was that made her so cool and made the other kids want to be around her. One day she invited me to a party at her house. Obviously, I said to myself, she's new and doesn't know that I'm an outcast and am never invited to parties. But I decided I would go anyway.

I was petrified as I knocked on the door, but she seemed genuinely glad to see me. She told me her parents weren't home and we went downstairs to a beautifully decorated family room in the basement. She introduced me to kids I recognized from school. I tried to talk with a few of them and discovered to my great surprise that it wasn't as hard as I thought it would be. After a few minutes, they all gathered in a circle and sat down in the middle of the floor. One boy pulled out a plastic bag that held something that looked like dried grass. Must be marijuana, I realized. I didn't know what was going on, so I kept my mouth shut, listened and watched. The boy put the marijuana in a cigarette paper, rolled it up, lit it and took a long drag before he passed it to the boy next to him. I watched the strange cigarette travel the circle. Each person breathed in deeply and held the smoke in their lungs for a long time. When the cigarette came around to me, I imitated what I had seen the others do, then I passed it to Brad, the boy sitting beside me. Within minutes I found myself laughing with Brad and not knowing why. Everything about him seemed so funny and I was feeling so good. Before I knew it, Brad was kissing and hugging me. I kept trying to get ahold of myself and figure out what was happening, but I liked the way I felt. I kept asking myself, doesn't he know who I am? Maybe he is new, too.

Brad and I began seeing each other regularly after that night. We would smoke marijuana and hang out at the pool hall. Sometimes we would take pills or mushrooms that made the world look garish and off-center, like a Vincent van Gogh painting. Brad taught me how to shoot pool and I became very good. He would arrange for me to play boys who didn't know how good I was, then he'd collect money after I'd win. I never thought too much about whether what we were doing was wrong. He liked me and I enjoyed having someone, anyone, in my life. I was too blinded by my needs to see where I was headed.

My grades began to fall and I was nearly dismissed from the Grapplerettes for showing up late or missing the meets entirely. All I cared about was getting high and forgetting everything.

But each time I came home I was haunted by the sight of my Bible sitting on the white dresser that my daddy had bought for me just before he died. It was one of the last remaining items from my old room. My friends and I had painted my pink bedroom pitch-black and installed a black light. The frilly pink bedspread and French Provincial bed had been abandoned. I now slept on a single mattress that floated in the middle of the room like an island in a sea of black. The Friday night drug parties had become as regular in my life as the Friday night youth meetings that they replaced. Many nights after I had stumbled into my room high on drugs, the last thing I saw before I closed my eyes was that Bible, just lying there. It was like an old friend who'd betrayed me and I rarely picked it up anymore. I felt I was punishing God by ignoring His word and getting back at Him for letting me down.

Mama was back home again. In a confined ward with supervision and on medication, she soon became docile and was judged by the doctors not to be dangerous. Still wrapped up in her own troubles, Mama didn't mind my odd comings and goings. Patch was trying to finish high school during the day and work a full-time job at night and wasn't aware of what I was up to.

One night I stumbled home feeling much worse than usual. I nearly fell up the two stairs that led to the kitchen, where Mom was sitting. I was thickheaded and I couldn't focus my eyes. I staggered toward my bedroom, mumbling that I didn't feel very well. I fell onto my mattress and the room began to spin. Large blots of colors in shimmering frog-green and flaming orange began to seep from the black walls and drip to the floor like candle wax. The pool of colors grew larger and spread toward me. The floor seemed to bubble and the ceiling expanded in and out, up and down. The whole room was undulating and I felt as if I were being tossed about in the belly of some great beast. I was nauseated, my arms and legs were weak, my fingers tingled and I couldn't feel my toes. The colors, the floor, the ceiling, all began to move faster, my body began to spin and I knew I was going to die.

From its place on my white dresser, the Bible seemed like a lifeline. I tried to grab it as I spun around the room, but I missed it at each pass. I felt a warm tear stream down my cheek. My mind raced to the tears I cried the day Pastor Montei hugged me. Something in me cried out to God. I grabbed my Bible and clutched it to my chest. I raised my fist toward the lurching ceiling and I screamed: "God, if You're so real, if all I read in this book is real, if all they told me at that church is real, then You save me now and I promise You I'll never touch drugs or alcohol again!"

Immediately the room became calm and a hush quieted my soul. I lowered my fist and grasped the quilt Grandma Jude had made me. I could feel the cloth and the stitches that held it together. I could feel the bubbly texture of the leather Bible. I could feel my toes, my fingers, my arms and legs, and I could feel a current of warm tears on my cheeks. I sat very still and tried to gather my bearings. I looked around the room. The colors had disappeared from the walls, the floor and the ceiling were still, I wasn't spinning and the nausea was gone. I looked at the Bible in my hand. I was surrounded by feelings of peace and love. I felt well and whole and I knew I had been delivered from the brink of death.

I awoke the next morning with my clothes on, my Bible in hand and Grandma Jude's warm quilt pulled to my neck. The sunlight streamed through my window and I could hear the faint sounds of Saturday morning cartoons coming from the family room. That morning brought a clarity that allowed me to put the pieces together. Someone had spiked my drink with drugs just for fun. It might have been a harmless prank if I had not taken so many drugs on my own. I realized that God had saved me from an overdose that surely would have killed me. It began to dawn on me that I had made a deal with God. I'd hidden marijuana in a ceramic pot in my room and felt a strong compulsion to get it. I didn't even take the time to comb my hair. I made my way to the bathroom, dumped the marijuana into the toilet, flushed it and watched the brown weeds swirl in the water, then disappear. Nervously I flushed again and again and again. I made my way back to my bedroom and picked up my Bible. For the first time I began to really talk to God, and this time the conversation was very different. Many times I had asked God, "Why?" Why did you let Daddy die? Why won't you make Mama better? Why did you let Grandma Jude die? Why did you take away Pastor Montei and my church family? But today I spoke to a friend, someone who I knew cared about me and about what happened to me, someone who was listening. For the first time since my father died I didn't feel alone. I understood in my heart that God was bigger than me and life itself and that He was always with me. All I had learned in church and had read in the Bible began to sink in that day. For the first time I saw God as my Heavenly Father and He felt warm and safe and loving, all the things Daddy was to me. I spent that Saturday nestled in God's love. I read my Bible, I slept peacefully, I gazed out of my window and really looked at the trees in the woods— they had never looked so green. A soft breeze filled my room. The birds sang sweeter and even the sky looked bigger. My hope expanded with the sky and my desire for a better life was not only restored but assured. I knew that with God's help, I would find it.

But I soon learned that my spiritual peace had created a social disaster. I didn't know how to tell my friends what had happened to me. That Friday I tried going to a party, but I knew I didn't belong there. I had no desire to drink or smoke marijuana. I didn't find conversations interesting. I walked home alone and sober from the last drug party I would ever attend. I raced to my bedroom to read my Bible and talk to God.

The end of summer was fast approaching and the prospect of starting school loomed before me like a black cloud. I didn't have drugs anymore, and I didn't have friends. What if I couldn't bring my grades back up? I began praying persistently. I dipped into the baby-sitting money I was saving and bought some clothes. At least I could try to look good, I thought.

I had discovered garage sales and secondhand stores. I spent hours in the bathroom experimenting with makeup and trying to arrange my stringy, static-stricken hair.

When school started, my old friends shunned me. We didn't have much in common anymore. I spent most of my time studying the Bible and keeping to myself. All that changed the day I saw Terry. I liked him immediately. Often I would stay after school to watch him practice basketball. He was confident, strong, at ease with himself, and he had lots of friends. Better yet, I'd heard he attended the Baptist Church. I could hardly believe it when he began to wait for me at the bus stop. A few days later he invited me to his house. I'd seen his family at baseball games and they seemed so "normal." I worried that I wouldn't know how to act. But I found his family warm, friendly and welcoming. Terry and I would talk for hours about all sorts of things. I'd tell him my dreams and how I loved to stay up and watch the sunrise. I thought for the first time in my life I might be in love.

One day we were at his house sitting on the couch and Terry began to rub my back, then moved his hand inside my blouse. I pushed him away and asked him to stop. He asked me why and I reached in my purse and handed him a card I'd picked up at church. It had a picture of Jesus on it and it said, "If you meet me and forget me you've lost nothing, but if you meet Jesus Christ and forget him you've lost everything."

"I want to give you this," I said. "It's the reason I want to live pure."

"I'll always carry it," Terry said, taking the card and putting it in his wallet.

One day Terry didn't show up at the bus stop. I nearly missed the bus waiting for him. I called his house as soon as I got home, but was told he wasn't there. I didn't see him in school the next day, but I waited for him at the bus stop anyway. As I scanned the parking lot, I saw Terry with another girl! A friend of Terry's saw me standing there and walked up to me.

"Terry found out what you really are: a druggie," he told me. "And Terry said he wasn't about to waste his time on a druggie."

I was crushed. When I got home I hid beneath Grandma Jude's quilt and sobbed for hours. I cried myself to sleep that night. But in the morning I awoke with a firm determination to show the world I certainly was not a druggie! I know who I am in God, even if no one else does.

It was so hurtful to see Terry at school. It was obvious that he was avoiding me.

God, I prayed, I just don't think I can go through dating. I don't seem to do well with boys, at least I haven't so far. You must have one boy You've picked out just for me. I'm going to work, study and pray hard and wait for him. I just don't think I can stand any more hurt. I want to think on things that are lovely like Your Word says. Help me think on things that are lovely, true, wise and of a good report.

I began to pray for my husband, too. Fervently, every night I'd talk with God about him. But something else was happening, something unexpected and wonderful. I didn't know whether it was my new clothes, my growing artistic ability that was being recognized or my brand-new soul, but kids, nice kids, were starting to talk to me and I was making friends.

One of my favorites was Mary Joseph, who had ten brothers and sisters and a mother who adopted anyone who came in the house. Mary's house was always filled with people and laughter and food, so much like my life before my father died. Ma Joseph loved me like a daughter, always asking if I'd eaten and how I was doing in school. She was the most talented seamstress I'd seen since Grandma Jude and she offered to teach me to sew. Half of her garage had been converted into her sewing room, where she turned out cheerleading uniforms, spangled outfits for baton twirlers or flowing wedding dresses. Nearly everyone in town had visited her little garage shop at one time or another. I loved going through the boxes of remnants, lace, buttons and trims. Ma Joseph's garage became my creative hideaway.

Often on weekends a group of teenagers would spend the night at the Josephs' home. One Friday night I found an unoccupied bed in the back room and tried to sleep but couldn't. I tossed and turned until long past midnight and decided to read, hoping it would make me sleepy. The house was quiet, the only sound the soft creaking of the wood floor as I made my way across the kitchen to the living room. I stepped over a curled figure in a sleeping bag and maneuvered past another sleeping body sprawled on one of the three couches. Quietly I made my way to an empty chair and wrapped myself in an afghan. The lamplight shone through the window and illuminated the edge of a Living Bible. A nice one, I thought. It looks brand-new. The spine of the book cracked as I opened it to I Corinthians, 13:4, reading, "Love is very patient and kind, never jealous or envious, never boastful or proud, never haughty or selfish or rude. Love does not demand its own way. It is not irritable or touchy. It does not hold grudges and will hardly even notice when others do it wrong. It is never glad about injustice, but rejoices whenever truth wins out. If you love someone you will be loyal to him no matter what the cost. You will always believe in him, always expect the best of him, and always stand your ground in defending him. . . . There are three things that remain—faith, hope, and love—and the greatest of these is love."

Lord, I began to pray, I love this passage. It brings me so much closer to You. I don't fully understand everything, but the words comfort me. Sometimes I feel like a child, then I feel like an adult and I feel lonely. Lord, I'll ask You again. Please don't make me go through dating in high school. It just doesn't seem to hold anything for me and I fear I will fall apart. You know me so well. I'm so fragile inside, Lord. Help me wait, Lord. Help me find the one You made just for me . . .

My prayer was interrupted by the sound of the front door lock clicking open. I glanced at the clock. It was 2:30 A.M.! Who could be coming in this late?

The outside lamp silhouetted a muscular figure, a man. The light shined in his face and I recognized Tom, one of Mary's older brothers.

"That's my Bible!" he spluttered. "What are you doing with my Bible?"

"Well, I can see you haven't read it very often," I snapped back. "It cracked when I opened it."

He looked amused and came toward me. In the dim light, I could see his smooth olive skin and black, shiny hair. He's cute, I thought, but I quickly pushed the idea away.

"What are you reading?" he asked.

I was surprised by his gentle voice. He was so muscular, I expected him to sound gruff, and his ill-tempered response to finding me reading his Bible had put me on guard.

"Oh, I opened to First Corinthians. I like to read the Bible."

"I'm going to go to the garage and lift weights. Would you like to come and read to me?"

"Sure. I mean, I guess."

I followed him and watched as he set up his weights. "Why are you coming in so late?"

"Oh, the disco just closed. I was out with my friend Tom Georgioff. He always closes the bar down."

The bar, I thought to myself, great. And he has a Bible that he doesn't read. Silently, in my thoughts, I began to pray. Great Lord, what's this? I asked.

Many times I've asked the Lord questions and the answers have come slowly. Sometimes they didn't come at all. But this time the answer was swift, an independent idea that appeared in my mind and, clearly, was not from me: This, my dear, will be your husband!

"What?" I protested out loud, and quickly looked at Tom to see if he had heard. But he was still assembling his weights and was paying me no attention. Silently I prayed. Lord, he's gentle, he looks pretty strong, but wait a minute, Lord, he's probably not even a Christian.

The answer was persistent: You heard Me, and you know Me by now. I said, he will be your husband.

Was I losing my mind? I always talked with God and He often talked back, but this was crazy. I'd only spoken a few words to this man. I'd only seen him once before that night. I tried to persuade myself that I was just up too late. I was just getting lonely. I just wanted someone in my life so desperately that I made it up. That's it, I made it up.

"Why are you lifting weights?" I asked.

"I compete in wrestling and I have to stay fit, even off-season. College will be tough and I'll need to be in top shape."

Fit he was, I thought as I watched his muscles bulge beneath the strain of the barbells. I was having trouble keeping my mind on the Bible reading. I'd never seen a man like this before. I was mesmerized by his broad, muscular chest and his powerful arms. I found my breathing irregular and I had to stop looking at him just to catch my breath.

I read to him from the Bible for a long time. When he finished lifting weights, he sat down on the floor next to me and we talked. Through the night we talked about many things. I felt so connected to this man, so at home sitting next to him. All too soon, streaks of light brightened the black sky. Sunrise was my favorite part of the day, but for the first time, it came much too soon. The sun was an intrusion, a blinding announcement that the night was over.

I had been embraced by such comfort and warmth talking to Tom, but the sun reminded me that good things in my life didn't last long.

Tom went away to Grand Rapids Junior College on a wrestling scholarship, promising to write back to me if I wrote to him. I entered high school and wrote to Tom nearly every week. When he answered, he talked to me like I was his kid sister, offering advice about everything, especially boys. He warned me to stay pure and not fall for the lies boys are sure to tell to get their way. What he didn't know was that I had come to believe God's words, that he was the one God had picked out for me and that I was saving myself for him.

MIXED
BLESSINGS

*"Though I walk in the midst of trouble,
you preserve my life."*

— P S A L M   1 3 8 : 7   (N I V)

The opportunities of high school spread out before me like a grand feast, and I sampled as much as I could. I had enjoyed the Grapplerettes so much in junior high that I went out for the high school squad and made it. We worked closely with Coach Bill Regnier, who was a hometown hero of sorts. Under his direction, our wrestling team had been the best in the state of Michigan for many years. We didn't know it then, but that winning streak would continue. Coach Regnier's coaching record for dual meets would stand at 500 wins, 57 losses and 3 ties by the end of his career, which stretched from 1965 to 1995. The coach and his wife, Carol, were Christians and had influenced many teenagers, including me and Tom, who had been one of the school's first state wrestling champions. The coach had brought Tom to a 44–0–0 wrestling record his senior year, which had helped Tom land a full-ride college scholarship in wrestling.

My head was nearly spinning with the newfound freedom that came with owning my very own car. As soon as Kenny and I turned fifteen, Patch explained our home situation to officials at the office of the Michigan Secretary of State and we were granted permission to take our driver's tests one year early. Mama was very supportive and faithfully drove us thirty miles for the classes. I had been saving my baby-sitting money since I was twelve years old and had stashed away $1,700. With most of that money and help from Mama, I bought a dusty-blue, 1972 clean-as-a-whistle Dodge Dart Swinger. Patch and my Great-Uncle Major, on my mama's side, who owned a gas station, helped me pick it out. It ran great except that every once in a while the starter wouldn't turn over. I didn't know a thing about cars, but Patch taught me that if I popped the hood and pushed a certain spot, the engine would jump to life. The boys at school really thought I knew what I was doing when I got beneath the hood. Boys were starting to notice me, and I was invited on many dates, but I turned down all of them. I firmly believed that God had given Tom to me and I was keeping my promise.

I took as many art classes as the school would allow and, in my sophomore year, discovered pottery, which became a lifelong love. As Ms. LaFrance taught the basics of working clay, I found myself making spiritual applications. In an artist's hands, a lump of clay begins as nothing but can end up as something spectacular. How true that is of our lives in God's hands, I thought. An artist must wedge and work the clay to strengthen it. Through our trials and tribulations, God works us to make us stronger.

Using recycled clay, which I loved to do, required a special touch. As I dug deep in the garbage, searching for the slimiest pieces of clay that someone else had thrown away, I thought about how often people are cast aside. As I slapped the clay onto the plaster wedging table, which would draw out the excess moisture, I thought about how God retrieves the abandoned, works them and makes them better than they had been before.

Timing is everything in working with recycled clay. If left on the plaster wedging table too long, the clay would harden and be impossible to work, not long enough and it's too watery. It wasn't long before I could tell when the clay was perfect. Then I wedged, or kneaded the clay, much like bread dough, before cutting it in half with a wire to check for air bubbles. A piece of pottery, however beautifully thrown, will explode inside the kiln if air is trapped inside the clay. This could happen to me, I thought. If I allow bitterness or anger to be trapped inside my heart, I could one day explode.

Ms. LaFrance was a wonderful teacher who took a personal interest in my work and allowed me to use the classroom during off hours. Many days I would go to school early, stay late or use my study period to bust clay or pound it until it was pliable, which proved to be terrific therapy when I was upset by my homelife.

I began to win awards for my art, especially my pottery. One of my pieces, an oriental-styled black and cream piece with red poppies, won a citywide competition sponsored by the Toledo Museum of Art. My piece was on display for weeks at the museum.

When the principal invited students to become involved in the after-school programs for underprivileged children, I jumped at the chance. Not only would I be able to share my art, but I wouldn't have to go home right after school. I volunteered to teach weaving and pottery to elementary students and found that they enriched my life as much as I hoped I touched theirs. I watched those little fingers struggle with the woof and warp of a loom and rejoiced with them when they finally found their rhythm. Who knew what their homelives were like and how much this minor success meant to their hearts?

I had found another outlet for my creativity and emerging leadership skills: community involvement. When I heard about the bicentennial celebration our town was organizing for 1976, I volunteered and participated in many events, including researching, designing and setting up a historical display in our library.

All those successes were spawning confidence, but it was during my sophomore year that my perception of myself completely turned around, and all because of the kind words of a classmate. Brett Holey, who was every girl's dream date, was one year ahead of me in school and had always been nice to me. As the president of the student council, it was Brett's job to count the ballots for homecoming queen. As I was getting books out of my locker one day, Brett came up to me with a big smile on his face.

"Leisha, I'm not supposed to tell you this, but you nearly won Sophomore Homecoming Queen Court," he said.

I began to laugh. "Stop it, Brett."

"No, Leisha, I'm serious. You lost by a few votes."

"Cut it out, that's not funny," I said, but I was still laughing.

"Leisha, I'm serious."

"You mean I was nominated? Really?"

"Nominated?" Brett grabbed me by the shoulders and made me look into his eyes. "Leisha, what I'm saying is you almost won. Don't you know how the other kids see you?"

I guessed I didn't. Brett was serious. He'd meant it. I'd almost won? Me? How could that be? I still kept mostly to myself at school. When other kids were out on dates, I was home reading my Bible. How did they see me? I wondered. But after that day, I walked a little taller and the boundaries I had unconsciously set for myself broadened. I suppose it shouldn't have been a surprise, then, when I received the letter that shook in my trembling hands as I tried to read it. I had to read it twice before the words sank in. I had been nominated to be a contestant in the Miss Teen USA beauty pageant, and would I be interested in participating? Would I ever!

"Mama, look at this," I said, unable to conceal the excitement in my voice.

"Oh, Leisha, how wonderful!" Mama answered, giving me a big hug. "You're so poised, so beautiful. You'll do great, I know you will. I've always said that you can do anything you set your mind to do."

I was thankful that this had happened during one of Mama's good times and that I could share the honor with her. With a car I had been able to give up baby-sitting to work at Lion's Department Store, one of Toledo's biggest and nicest. I was working in the teenage clothing department and was having fun helping girls my own age pick out beautiful clothes. When the store manager heard of my nomination, he suggested that the store sponsor me and provide me with the outfits I would need to compete.

What a blessing that was. I picked out some beautiful clothes, including an off-white evening dress with a flowing skirt and spaghetti shoulder straps. A matching shawl was tossed over one shoulder and tied beneath the opposite arm, much like the title banner that the winning girl would wear.

The pageant was held just after my junior year in high school, at the Hilton Hotel in Kalamazoo, Michigan. Mama and I made the trip together, and as soon as we got there, we peeked in the ballroom and giggled together like girlfriends. Oh, how the crystal chandeliers sparkled. I savored the vision of the most elegant room I had ever seen, and I wondered, does Cinderella really get to go to the ball?

I gave a speech on patriotism and the importance of volunteer work, which seemed to be received well. I felt like a princess in my diaphanous gown as I smiled broadly and wet my teeth as I had been instructed, and waited for my name to be called. The walk down the runway seemed exceedingly long. Blinded by the bright lights and uncomfortable in the unfamiliar high heels, I began to pray, Lord, just don't let me fall off my shoes.

Onstage, many of us linked arms as we waited to hear the judges' decision. I was thinking how wonderful the experience had been. What a thrill just to be here, I thought. As the master of ceremonies began to announce the runners-up, I was jolted out of my thoughts.

"Third runner-up, Leisha Miller!"

That sounded like my name. Did I hear right? I hesitated, frozen in place. The girls around me pushed me forward and I hesitantly took my place on the winner's platform. It was the last place I expected to be.

I took home two large trophies, one for third runner-up and the citizenship award for outstanding contribution in my community. I never learned who had nominated me.

Everything had been going well. Senior year was going to be my year, I just knew it. Tom and I had been writing on a regular basis and slowly, and much to his surprise, our relationship had changed. I'd gone from kid sister to romantic interest and we'd officially started dating during his school breaks. While I could hardly wait for those visits, they showed me that Tom was unsure about our relationship. His letters were chatty and warm, but in person he was quiet and reserved. Tom was struggling between doing what he knew was right and doing what felt good, and my prayers for him intensified.

Often I'd be at his house visiting Mary when Tom got ready to go out on the town. I knew he was seeing other girls, but I didn't lecture or complain. I ironed his clothes for him, prayed and counted on God to change his heart.

Tom had transferred to Toledo University, which was not far from my house. Frequently I would take raw clay to his dorm room and work on a pottery piece while he studied. We never talked much, we just enjoyed being together. On my way to Tom's dorm room late one afternoon, I slowed for the speed bump at the campus entrance and saw Tom's Volkswagen Beetle approaching. As he slowed for the bump, my heart fluttered as I saw blond hair in the passenger seat.

"Hi, where are you going?" I said as cheerfully as I could.

Tom looked dismayed. His face was a blend of befuddlement, annoyance and a little bit of guilt. Suddenly my spirit was amused at God's timing. What were the odds of us meeting at the speed bump? Instead of becoming angry, I began to chuckle.

"I was just taking her home," Tom said.

Sure, I thought. Tom asked me to meet him at his dorm room, and as I drove on, I wondered what explanation he was giving to the poor girl.

I was working on my pottery when Tom walked through the door. He was very quiet and I didn't say a word either, leaving Tom's lecture up to God. When we finally talked, Tom confessed that he and the blonde, who was a member of the volleyball team, had been planning a date. He wondered why every time he tried to plan something without including God, he got caught.

"Remember how powerful prayer is" was my only response.

Tom didn't really understand my faith. We had been trying to find a church that suited both of us for some time. Tom had been brought up a Catholic and I was willing to convert if that was God's plan for my life, but I didn't know much about Catholicism. I was overwhelmed with the beauty and pageantry of the service, but the rituals were foreign to me and I wanted to know the meanings behind each one. Why did Tom dip his hand in water and cross himself?

"Shhh . . . I don't know. We'll talk later."

Why did he kneel down and cross himself again before entering a pew?

"I don't know, just do it."

Why couldn't I go to communion with him? What was the incense for? I asked about everything because there was so much I didn't understand.

On the way home in the car Tom told me he didn't know why he did all those things.

"You mean you perform all those rituals and you don't know why, but you just keep doing them?" I didn't understand how anyone could just do something for the sake of doing it and not know the meaning behind it.

"I don't know," Tom said. "I guess you have to be a Catholic to understand. Ask my mom, she'll know why."

"Tom, you mean you have done these things all your life and you don't know why? How can you do that? Don't you want to know what it all means?"

"Well, of course, but I just can't explain it."

"Then why should I go to Mass with you? Why should I consider becoming a Catholic? God is very real to me!"

We rode the rest of the way in silence, each pondering the words of the other. The resolution, it seemed, would elude us yet another day.

At home, my brothers and I had become accustomed to ducking the shrapnel from Mama's illness, but we were learning that the sharpest pieces were yet to hit. Mama had taken up with an older man, he must have been in his fifties, and he began to spend a great deal of time at our house. We were put off by his appearance, which would have won him last-place honors in an Elvis Presley impersonator contest. Rich never took off the large, dark sunglasses that he wore, even inside the house. Heavy oil weighted down his slick blond hair, and his stomach bulged beneath skintight polyester shirts and pants. His thick leather belt bore an enormous buckle that was choked with colored glass cut in the shape of jewels. What bothered us more than never being able to look him in the eye was that his stories were never the same twice. My brothers and I feared that a con man had attached himself to Mama, but persuading her of that was another matter.

"He loves me," she would protest. "You just can't stand that I have someone in my life."

"Mama, we're afraid he's trying to take advantage of you," I said.

"How? Just answer me that. He loves me."

The "how" part of her question seemed obvious to everyone but Mama. Rich began to talk to Mama about taking a trip to Tennessee, where, if she moved quickly, she could buy an interest in a hotel that was sure to be a moneymaker. He was certain of it. Why, he intended to invest himself just as soon as he received a check that should be coming any day now. Hey, wait a minute, maybe she could put in money for both of them and he could pay her back. Yeah, that was the ticket! They wouldn't have to wait around for his check, they could go down to Tennessee right away! What a wonderful idea, said my mama.

One day he and Mama rolled up in front of the house in a brand-new special anniversary edition of the Lincoln Continental. It was called the Diamond Jubilee and among other lavish features, displayed simulated diamonds that had been laminated in both of the rear opera windows. At a time when the comparable Cadillac Eldorado sold for $11,900 loaded, and a Ford Mustang II Ghia cost $3,972 off the assembly line, the Diamond Jubilee's sticker price was $20,529. The moon roof and leather interior cost extra. A total of 5,159 Diamond Jubilees were sold that year.

"Look what your mama bought me so we could go to Tennessee in style!" said Rich. "Let's all go for a ride."

Reluctantly my brothers and I piled in the backseat. I looked through the back window where phony diamonds floated in the middle of the small opera windows and sparkled in the sun. Disgusted by the pretense and extravagance, I rolled my eyes at Patch.

Patch leaned over and whispered so that only I could hear. "Have a good time, Leisha. You're riding in your college education."

We pulled Mama aside and tried to tell her our fears about Rich, but she would hear none of it. She accused us of trying to cause trouble and kill her chance for happiness. The tension in our house mounted until the day Mama came home from her regular psychiatrist appointment with news for me.

"My psychiatrist says I should get rid of anything in my life that is hurting me or holding me back, and that is you," she told me. "Get out."

"Mama, what do you mean? Why are you blaming me? I've tried so hard to be a good daughter. I've tried so hard to please you."

"You're not my daughter," she hissed. "If you don't want to accept the way I am, or the way I want to live, get out!"

"Mama, how can you say that?"

"Get out!" she screamed. "I want you out of my life!"

Then she walked to the silverware drawer and pulled out a foot-long butcher knife as calmly as if she intended to chop vegetables for dinner. But she was pointing the knife at me, and she was coming toward me.

"You're no daughter of mine," she said, over and over again, her face contorted, her eyes wild and strange.

"Mama, please, no!" I pleaded, but I could see it was no use. She kept coming. I ran down the steps into the family room, out the door to the garage, and jumped into my car. I shut the door as fast as I could and locked it behind me. I nearly flooded the engine trying to start it. Thankfully it kicked over and I sped away, spewing a wave of gravel in my wake.

I drove for the longest time, not knowing where to go. I was too ashamed to confide in anyone except Tom, and he was living in a college dormitory. I had never talked about my homelife to anyone else, not even Coach, so who could be expected to understand this strange situation? I figured I would just have to find another place to live. I pulled into an apartment complex and walked into the manager's office and inquired about renting an apartment. If I didn't spend too much on food or utilities, my pay at the Lion's store might cover the rent. I might be able to find a roommate, I reasoned. But the manager looked at me as if I were trying to make him the butt of some joke.

"You're barely old enough to drive, you can't rent an apartment," he said.

I got back in my car and put my head on the steering wheel. O dear Lord, I prayed, what should I do? Where should I go? I drove around until after dark and found myself at Ma Joseph's house. She opened the door, wrapped her comforting arms around me and told me I was always welcome and could stay as long as I needed to. That's where Patch found me the next day.

"Don't worry, I'm going to take care of you," he said, giving me a big bear hug.

Since Patch was an adult and had a full-time job, he could rent a place for both of us. But the only place we could afford, even after pooling our money, was a tumbledown one-bedroom shack in the roughest part of town. The foundation must have been bad because all the floors tilted. Walking toward the back of the living room was like walking uphill, which often made me feel dizzy, but I was grateful for a place to sleep.

I sneaked back home when Mama wasn't there and hurriedly packed my clothes. This was the first time we kids had been split up, and Patch and I missed our brothers, but we talked to them as often as we could. The boys told us that Rich and Mama had been fighting because he wanted Mama to sign the deed of the house over to him, and she wouldn't do it.

A few days later the house our father built mysteriously caught fire. It's lucky that no one had been home at the time, the firefighter told Patch. They couldn't determine the cause of the fire but knew that it had started in the basement. The house would easily have burned to the ground, but neighbors saw smoke and had alerted them in time. The hollowed-out shell of what had been our home looked so forlorn to Patch and me. Everything I had left behind, my entire collection of Barbie dolls and their clothes, artwork that I had saved, pictures of our father, were gone. What survived intact, however, was a large pile of boxes that Rich had stored in our garage.

"What do you think, should we look in them?" I asked.

"Maybe we should," Patch said. "We don't know what he's keeping here. What if it's something illegal?"

We didn't have to look far before we found the evidence that confirmed our suspicions. Rich had a little black book that contained names and addresses of wealthy widows all over the country. Notations in the margins read, "$200,000 estate," or "Two homes and four cars, including Mercedes." Rich, it seemed, was a gigolo who made his living stealing the legacy of dead men from the lonely women they left behind. But our proof came too late. Mama was nowhere to be found.

We were relieved to learn that the house wasn't a total loss and could be repaired. I was amazed that despite all he had to worry about, Patch had made sure the insurance on our home had been paid. Kenny and Joey moved into the little shack with us and Patch arranged to have our home rebuilt. We were so happy to be together once more.

A few days after the fire, Rich drove the Diamond Jubilee up to the door of our rental. From inside the house, Patch saw him, grabbed the baseball bat and ran for the door. Rich saw him coming.

"Hey, hey!" Rich yelled, sprinting back to his car. "I don't want no trouble. I just want to know where your mama's at."

"I can't believe you're here," Patch yelled at him. "You step one foot inside this house and I'll kill you."

I had grabbed onto Patch's arm and was trying to pull him back in the house. "Patch, don't do it. He's not worth it. You'll end up in jail," I pleaded. For the first time Patch frightened me. I had never seen fire in his eyes like that. "We don't know where Mama is," I yelled to Rich. "Patch! Please, don't do it!"

Patch wrestled free of me and ran into the street, missing Rich only by seconds. We all stood in the street and watched the taillights of the Diamond Jubilee growing dim in the darkness.

Despite the new troubles, or maybe because of them, I threw myself into school and community activities, leaving home early, staying late, volunteering for every interesting or worthy project and working at the Lion's store every weekend. Life at home was chaotic, unpredictable, but school was solid, logical, an environment that could be understood and even enjoyed. In fact, it seemed as if God used school to make up for what I lacked at home. Brett's words, it seemed, were prophetic. I was elected homecoming queen that year by a vote of the entire student body. As the crown was placed on my head in front of the cheering crowd during halftime, I thought back to how surprised I'd been two years earlier just to be nominated. That night I felt overwhelmed and honored. I thanked God that He had brought me so far from those dark pool hall days. As I prayed, I felt God impress upon me Proverbs 22:1: "A good name is more desirable than great riches; to be esteemed is better than silver or gold."

One afternoon I was sitting in the bleachers watching basketball practice when out of the blue, Terry, my junior high school crush, ran up the stairs and sat beside me.

"Do you still watch sunrises?" he asked.

"Yes, I still love to," I answered.

That's all he said, but he looked into my eyes for a long time. For one brief moment, I caught a glimpse of what could have been between us. Then he was gone.

I didn't see much of Terry after that. But shortly after we exchanged those brief words, a friend called to tell me that Terry and several other boys had been in a car accident and that Terry hadn't made it. I could hardly bring myself to walk into the funeral home. Many of my classmates were crying on each other's shoulders as I slowly walked up to his casket. His hands were crossed over his chest and in one of them he held a small card that read, "If you meet me and forget me you've lost nothing, but if you meet Jesus Christ and forget him you've lost everything."

My knees buckled and I had to grab a chair to keep my balance.

"They found that card in his wallet," someone behind me said.

Could it be? Had he carried the card I had given him all that time? I would never know.

A few months later, my classmates elected me Snowball Queen of the Winter Ball and president of the senior class. I landed a spot on the yearbook staff and was quickly named editor. And I received another letter inviting me to compete in the Miss Teen USA pageant, which would be held in July 1979, one month after high school graduation. And all that time I had spent studying had paid off. I was graduating in the top of my class. I was on top of the world. I thanked God for all these wonders, but I wondered, why me? As I questioned, I began to understand that God honors us for His sake, not ours. When He gives us a good name, it is to be used to influence others for Him, and I vowed to honor His purpose for my life. By the time I was elected prom queen, the repairs had been completed and we moved back into the house Dad had built for us. Living in that dilapidated shack made me appreciate our lovely home all the more.

Patch would get home from the factory quite late and I would often awaken to find him at the kitchen table poring over the bills. We were just squeaking by with what Patch made and the small Social Security check that we received from our father's account. The check came directly to us because Mama had gone to court a few months before she had left and given Patch legal custody of us children. It wasn't easy, but the four of us were getting by, and so I was not prepared when I answered a knock at the door to find Mama standing on our porch. Everything about her looked dirty, her matted hair, her legs, her feet which had no shoes, her torn and stained dress, her face, blackened with dirt. She looked as if she had been sleeping in the streets. I felt my face blaze with anger. How dare she show up here? Without a word, I slammed the door in her face. The Holy Spirit immediately spoke to my heart and I was convinced that what I had done was wrong. The thought flew into my mind: Regardless of what she has done, she is your mother, honor her.

I slowly opened the door to see her still standing there, crying, and compassion crept into my heart. I let her in and she walked right back into our lives.

Mama had been on the road with Rich for months, never spending much time in any one place. It was in New York where she'd found a psychiatrist who had finally diagnosed her correctly. She suffered from manic-depressive disorder, a debilitating combination of prolonged, euphoric, emotional highs, which are often accompanied by wild spending sprees, and long stretches of deep, dark depression. It's much like riding an emotional roller coaster through life, and you always knew that every few months, that great big old hill would be coming up again. When we learned the symptoms, we wondered how so many other doctors had missed it. For the first time, Mama was responding well, really well, to a drug. Lithium controlled Mama's disorder, leveling the unstable emotional peaks and valleys into a peaceful plain, leaving her calm and in control.

At first we were skeptical. After all, we had seen brief periods of remission only to watch Mama fall harder than the time before. But this time she didn't resort to her old patterns. She was trying hard to join in family life and she seemed to grow steadily better. Soon she was able to take on small tasks around the house, such as washing dishes and, later, grocery shopping.

Mama said it was in the grocery line that she realized she was getting better. A magazine caught her eye, and for the first time in years, Mama found herself wanting to read a story promoted on the cover. But a decade of electric shock treatments that jarred her brain and prolonged use of heavy medication had left Mama permanently frail and obliterated most of her memories.

Each of us had issues to work through with Mama, but we couldn't because she didn't remember any of the things she had done. My heart cried for her as she struggled to salvage bits and pieces from the past. Whenever some harsh deed flashed back to her, she would sit and cry and apologize over and over again.

We understood that what had happened to her, to all of us, was not her fault. Just as no one would purposely choose cancer, Mama didn't choose mental illness. But because this illness causes unacceptable behavior, those who suffer from it don't get the compassion that cancer victims get. Instead, they often receive harsh judgment from those who confuse mental illness with character flaws.

Mama had sworn that she would never forgive Patch for committing her to a state mental hospital, but she did. And I forgave her for chasing me away. We all forgave each other. Forgiveness took on new depth and meaning for all of us.

The biggest shock, however, was learning that Mama had come home to us flat broke. Many others had already taken advantage of Mama's condition. She had been partners in many failed ventures over the years. But it was still a shock to learn that in less than ten years, Mama had gone through Dad's entire estate. Though Dad had left enough money for a college education as well as a start for each of us children, our only remaining valuable was the home that had nearly burned to the ground.

The enormity of the situation overwhelmed me. I just wanted out. I couldn't wait to graduate from high school, get out and find the life God intended me to live. I believed with all my heart I would find it with Tom. It was understood that we would marry someday, but it hadn't been discussed. Graduation was only weeks away when Tom brought it up. He told me how much he loved me and that he wanted to spend the rest of his life with me. He suggested we not wait, but that we marry shortly after I graduated from high school. At first I was thrilled. This is what I had been waiting for, this is why I'd not dated and waited patiently for him to settle down. But the euphoria quickly dissolved and my spirit became troubled. I was completely confused. What's wrong with me? I demanded of myself. This makes no sense at all. Am I afraid? Am I scared this will be too good and disappear, too? God, I asked, what is this all about? And Scripture began to appear in my mind.

"Have nothing to do with the fruitless deeds of darkness but rather expose them" (Ephesians 5:11).

I argued, Wait a minute, God, I know he's not a Christian, but You picked him out for me. More Scripture answered my protests.

"Do not be unequally yoked with unbelievers. What fellowship has righteousness with lawlessness? And what communion has light with darkness?" (2 Corinthians 6:14).

I opened my mouth to speak and, like Tom, could hardly believe the words came from my mouth. "I can't marry you."

"What? Why on earth . . ."

"Because I can't be unequally yoked with a non-Christian. It will never work." And I explained the biblical concept of being "unequally yoked." A farmer should never hitch a yoke to a mule and a horse and expect them to pull a plow together, because the animals are too different. The horse might start off walking while the mule decides to sit in the middle of the field. If the plow went anywhere at all, it would be in circles.

I will never forget the look on Tom's face. He was as confused as I was. Hadn't I waited all this time for him? He quietly walked away and I quietly wanted to die.

I didn't see him for three days. No one did. On the third day I was beginning to worry when Mary asked if I'd seen him. I began to silently pray, O God, please, I need to know if I did the right thing . . . but the ringing telephone interrupted my prayer.

"Hello" was all Tom said, but I could tell by his voice he was different.

"You've been with the Lord, haven't you?"

"Yes," he said.

Tom had spent the entire three days alone with God. He had cried and wept and experienced a life-changing event where God showed him every rotten thing he had ever done to me, and how, despite it all, I was faithful in my love for him. Tom cried over every sin, every trespass, he had ever committed against another person, and he had repented and dedicated his life entirely to God.

As I heard Tom's story, I saw God's plan with crystal clarity. In turning down Tom's proposal, I had taken an unfathomable risk. I had denied the yearnings of my heart and, instead, followed God's leading. And what I had learned from that experience was that God will be faithful, that He is in control. I knew at that moment that I must always do what I know to be right, despite the feared consequences, and even when it doesn't make sense. I learned to trust God that day. And in my obedience, God had given me the desires of my heart. I was free to marry my love.

Chapter 5

ROAR
OF THE
RIGHTEOUS

*"The wicked man flees though no one
  pursues,
but the righteous are as bold as a lion."*

— PROVERBS 28:1 (NIV)

Our high school orchestra filled the auditorium with the majesty of Edward Elgar's "Pomp and Circumstance" as I confidently walked across the stage to receive my diploma. This special day marked the beginning of my real life, the life God had planned for me. I just knew the worst was over.

My SAT scores had been good enough to land me a scholarship to study art, but after hearing that I planned to be married, my dismayed guidance counselor had tried unsuccessfully to talk me out of marriage.

"Think about your future!" she had shouted at me. "Don't throw your life away like this."

But nothing could shake my firm belief that Tom was my future. I assured her I would use the scholarship after we were married. As Tom and I planned our wedding, I silently sent up a tentative plea to God: "Surely I can be happy now . . ."

Weddings and beauty pageants certainly can keep a girl shopping. On the day before the Fourth of July, I was driving to Bargain City Shopping Plaza in nearby Toledo while thinking about where Tom and I would go to watch the fireworks the next night.

I hadn't been able to start my car that day, so Mom let me take hers. I pulled my mom's 1972 Plymouth Fury into the crowded parking lot and couldn't find a place near the door, so I headed to the outskirts. Come on, I chided myself, the walk will do you good.

I bounded to the door of the mall in anticipation. I was days away from the Miss Teen USA pageant and was in search of a pair of white knee-high boots and matching stockings for the red, white and blue costume I planned to wear when I delivered my speech on patriotism.

I had worked hard on this pageant. Every word was memorized, every move was staged and fixed in my mind. This would be my last chance to compete before my wedding made me ineligible. I didn't expect to win, but I thought participating in the pageant would be a great pre-wedding adventure and I could someday tell our children.

I made my way through the crowds to the shoe department and was surprised to find boots in my size so quickly. Just as fast, I found matching stockings and headed for the door.

I needed to hurry home so I would be ready when Tom arrived later with the new van that we had just purchased to begin our lives together.

Tom had driven to Detroit to show off the new van to his brothers and would be returning soon. In a few days, Pam Ansted, another contestant from my hometown, and I planned to drive to Kalamazoo, where the competition would be held. I could hardly wait to show Pam my new boots.

As I walked through the doors of the mall into the parking lot, I was so caught up in my excitement that I nearly forgot which car I had driven. I put my hand up to shield my eyes from the blinding sunlight that bounced up from the asphalt and looked around. In the distance, I spotted Mom's old car. Oh yeah, I sighed, contrasting the vision before me with the shiny, sleek van that I would soon be driving. From where I stood, Mom's car looked like an abandoned tank, its drab, olive-green paint dented and speckled with rust.

I walked across the lot, hopped in and fumbled for the keys, which were, as usual, lost in the tangle inside my purse. I won't have to drive this many more times, I thought, fishing the keys from the bottom of my purse and putting them into the ignition.

UUrrr . . . UUrrr . . . The arthritic engine lurched twice, but refused to turn over. I tried again. *UUrrr . . . UUrrr . . .*

I looked around and noticed a Pizza Hut across the parking lot. I began to hunt around in my purse for a dime, realizing I would have to call one of my brothers and ask him to come and pick me up. Suddenly a man appeared by my door.

"You seem to be having some trouble. Can I help?" he asked. He was about twenty-two years old, and he had a strong, athletic build. He seemed so friendly, so gentlemanly, so normal. He smiled reassuringly at me. I thought of my Tom. This is the kind of thing Tom would do, I thought, help a lady in distress. God has sent an angel to help me.

"Thanks," I said. "But I don't want to inconvenience you."

"Oh, no trouble at all," he said. "I'll check under the hood. I know a thing or two about cars. Maybe I can save you the money a tow truck would charge." He grinned at me as he walked to the front of the car, popped the hood and disappeared beneath it.

"Try to start it now," he shouted.

I turned the ignition key. *UUrrrr . . . uurrrr* came the unhealthy grinding beneath the hood as the ailing engine refused to budge.

Darn my mom's old car, I thought. I began to wonder what a tow truck would cost and how much we would have to spend to fix the engine.

He moved quickly and smoothly from the front of the car and knelt down inside my open door. Suddenly he lurched toward me. While my mind raced to make sense of what was happening, I felt the cold, hard barrel of the gun he shoved into my ribs.

O my God, I thought. *O my God. No!* This can't be happening. Not now. Not now. Oh please, *oh please.* But it was happening and the terror of the moment consumed me, stealing away my breath. I struggled to breathe, but my heart felt like a heavy stone pushing against my lungs.

My heart was pounding so fiercely that I feared my chest would explode. I gasped for air.

"Move over," he ordered, shoving the gun harder into my ribs.

I slid to the passenger side and he eased onto the driver's seat and closed the door. Craning his neck, he surveyed the parking lot quickly, then he shoved the steel barrel of the gun into my neck.

"Get in the backseat," he snarled. "Now!"

I threw my leg over the back of the long, bench front seat and tumbled over it. I landed hard between the floor and the backseat and struggled to right myself. He was upon me in a flash, shoving me on my back and holding me down with one muscular arm while his other hand jammed the gun into my throat.

O Lord, I began to cry out in my mind. No. No. No. I know what is coming, Lord, no, please no.

He shoved me backward, knocking me against the seat and hurling my mind beyond the horror of the moment into the horrors of the past. Scenes jumbled together in an indistinguishable tangle of pain and grief.

> *I am a little girl and my daddy's voice booms from the*
> *front door: "Where's my princess?" he demands, as if he can't*
> *see me racing to meet him. "Where's my princess?"*
> *"Here I am!" I cry as I throw my arms around his legs*
> *and hug the only part of him I can reach.*

From somewhere, he pulled out a roll of white, medical tape, yanked free about a foot of it and began to bind my hands together in front of me. Around and around my wrists he wound the tape, each time the rigid, unforgiving tape cutting deeper into my skin, halting the flow of blood to my hands. He jerked the tape to his mouth and tore it off the roll with his teeth.

He pushed the gun deep into my throat and straddled me. With the pressure of the gun pinning me to the seat, his other hand expertly unbuckled his belt, unzipped the zipper and pulled down his blue jeans faster than I thought was possible. I prayed in my heart, in my head and in my spirit, a torrent of unintelligible moanings and groanings understood by no one but God.

His hostile and determined face swam above me. The smile was gone. In its place was a hardened grimace. His eyes became slits. I could see the pores of his skin, feel his breath on my face, my neck, as he shoved me back.

My eyes focused on a small triangle tear in the ceiling upholstery. It seemed so far above me, like it was at the end of a long, narrow tunnel. I never knew that was there. Of course not, I argued, I'd never been thrown down in the backseat before. How could I be thinking something so trivial? my mind demanded of itself.

He yanked me from my thoughts as he grabbed my blouse, my favorite yellow and black pinstriped blouse. The gauzy fabric ripped easily in his powerful hands. He jerked the front of my pants open, yanked at the zipper and tried to pull them off of me.

The zipper hadn't fully been lowered and the yellow slacks lodged at my hips.

"Take them off," he demanded. With my wrists bound together, removing my pants was a struggle. I pushed them down, one leg at a time until they were off, and I kicked them to the floor. The sticky vinyl upholstery adhered to the back of my legs.

He grabbed my panties and ripped them off of me. For a second he loomed above, powerful and menacing, and then he was upon me.

He pressed upon me, his full weight driving down upon me, and I was overcome with the heaviness of him and with the strong nauseating stench of sweet, cheap cologne, rancid sweat and marijuana.

There's a man in my room. He is outlined by the light
from the porch lamp that shines through my curtains. He lies
on top of me, mumbling something through his liquor breath.

*He moves around all over me and places his rough hands on
me. I keep my eyes shut in horror. I roll over as if still asleep,
hoping he will leave. He doesn't leave. I think his weight will
crush me.*

Not since I was a child had I felt the pure oppression an intrusive body could inflict. The prickle of the hair on his legs, his chest, and his damp skin pressing down made my skin crawl and my stomach lurch. This time it was daylight. I couldn't curl up in a little corner of darkness and hide. I couldn't pull quilts over my head and pretend it was a bad dream. Beneath the witness of the glaring sun, this could not be denied.

Surely someone will see, I thought. This is a busy parking lot in the middle of the day, surely someone will make him stop. My next breath could be my very last. I could be gone in a blink of an eye.

*Three large men are struggling with Mama. She is
screaming and kicking and fighting as they force a white
straitjacket around her arms. They tie her up so she can't
move. They bind her legs so she can't kick. I began to scream
at the sight. "What are you doing to my mother?" I cry to
them. "Leave her alone."*

I was losing feeling in my fingers, my hands were going numb. I struggle against him and he raises a powerful fist over my face. But the thrusting of the gun deep into my throat stills me and he lowers his hand. There is a silencer on the gun. I know he is serious. The gun feels cold and hard and final.

*Street evangelist David Wilkerson is preaching the gospel
when gang leader Nicky Cruz screams at him to shut up or he
will cut him up in a million pieces.*

*Wilkerson is calm and brave: "Go ahead and every piece
will continue to love you."*

Oh, if only I could have faith like that, I think to myself.

I tried desperately to push him off. He sneered at my feeble
efforts. He was twice my size and immovable. Pushing against him
was like trying to move a mountain. Frantically I dug my fingernails
into his legs, trying desperately to fight any way I could. A shift of
his body and my hands were immobilized, paralyzed beneath his
heaviness. There is nothing I can do. My mind squirmed in terror, as
my spirit cried out to God.

*Everyone in church is mad at everyone else and especially
mad at the pastor and I am again left adrift. I fall in with
the wrong crowd. I take drugs. Someone slips something in my
drink and I overdose and know I am going to die. I pray to
the God who once guided me. If You are real, help me now.
Help me, heal me, and I promise I will never take drugs
again, I challenge Him.*

In an instant I am sober.

I screamed and kicked at the window, praying that someone
would see, frantic for someone to stop this horror, aching for someone to come to my defense. A middle-aged man and woman walked
by. The woman's graying hair was pulled tightly in a bun on the top
of her head. They heard my screams and looked into the car. I kick
frantically at the window, desperate for them to see. He saw them
and halted my kicking by twisting my leg downward at an unnatural
angle. Pain shot through my leg and hip like fire.

They couldn't have missed the gun. Stop! Please stop, I screamed
in my mind as I watched them glance in my window. They see! They
see what is happening! But my heart is as broken as my body as I

watch them get into the car next to mine and drive away. Why won't you help me? I would help you! I plead, but it's too late. They are gone.

God talks to me with 2 Timothy 4:16, which reverberates through my mind: "At my first defense, no one came to my support, but everyone deserted me. May it not be held against them. But the Lord stood at my side and gave me strength . . ."

Oh, be my strength, my God, my spirit cried out.

I am in high school. God is faithful and has turned my life around. I am an honor student, the homecoming queen, the president of the senior class. I am headed for college with an academic scholarship.

He sat on my chest and the crushing weight of him forced the air out of my lungs. I couldn't breathe. I was wild with fear. Any moment he could crash through my chest, every bone collapsing upon itself, piercing through my lungs, crushing my heart, taking my life.

I am eighteen, a finalist in the Miss Teen USA beauty pageant, months away from marrying a godly young man, and I am being raped. O my God, I am being raped.

Time, no longer constant and dependable, became fluid. It suspended eerily as the seconds stretched out and lasted far longer than seemed possible. He assaulted my body in every way imaginable for what seemed like hours.

The terror in my heart was unbearable. The prayers I had mumbled in my spirit began to fly out of my mouth, loudly. I began to loudly cry to the only One who, throughout my life, had been a constant source of love, comfort and strength. I began to loudly pray to the Living God.

"Father," I began to cry out loud, "I need You. I need You right now."

He became enraged that I was praying out loud, and shoved the gun harder into my neck. *"Shut up!"* he screamed.

But I continued to pray with all the strength within me. "Lord, I need You now!! Be with me now!!" I screamed the prayer.

"What *are* you?" he hissed at me angrily.

"I'm a Christian," I said.

"Don't give me that, I've been that route before," he said. "You're a real Bible booker, aren't you? *Shut up.* Don't say another word."

His threat loomed in the air pregnant with fatal implications of what would come if I disobeyed. I looked at the silencer. I knew he would shoot me and leave me there. But I continued to pray and I prayed even louder.

"Lord, be with me now. Stay by my side, Lord, be with me, comfort me, fill me . . . O Lord I need You *now."*

As the words left my mouth, I immediately felt the presence of the Holy Spirit. It filled the car and I felt a strength I'd never before known.

He shoved the gun into my neck so hard that my head lurched painfully back.

"Shut up!" he screamed. "Shut up or I'm going to blow you into a million pieces."

As soon as he said "million pieces," a calmness washed over me.

If I am certain of anything in this life, it is that God gave me the words that flew out of my mouth before I had a chance to think about them. Before I had a chance to wonder if they were the right thing to say. Before I could think or rationalize or theorize. Before I had a chance to rely on my own power. God took over and filled me with His power. He gave me the only words that could have saved my life. The tiny seeds that began as David Wilkerson's words, planted by God in the recesses of my mind at a Christian youth retreat so many years ago, had taken root.

"Go ahead," I said calmly and with all the authority that God had poured out upon me. "Go ahead, and every piece will continue to love you. Every piece will cry out, 'God loves you!' "

His mouth flew open and he was stunned into silence. Then his face began to contort and he began to tremble and shake. He looked puzzled, confused, and at the same time horrified. For a moment I felt a twinge of compassion for him. He had met someone he had never before encountered: the Spirit of the Living God.

I'd been a Christian for years but I had never in my life felt the presence of the Holy Spirit like I did in that car. I don't think I've known such strength as I did at that moment, realizing in a very human way that the power of the Living God resides in us and is real.

It didn't make one bit of sense for me to tell my violent attacker that God loved him. But in my heart, I know I walked in obedience for one minute and He saved my life.

We can't equip our daughters or sons any better for this world than with the Spirit of the Living God. Neither a gun, nor karate, nor all the self-defense techniques known to man could have helped me at that moment. But the Spirit of the Living God was faithful to me and saved my life.

God had clearly taken over. The man who a few moments before had loomed above me so powerfully under his own strength was now frightened, weak and trembling in the presence of the Almighty God. He must have sensed that he was no longer in control. He lost all sexual desire, and all he wanted was to be out of that car. He fumbled with his gun, waving it at me, his face trembling.

"You get down in the floor right here and don't you look up. If you do, I will blow your head off. I know you. I know your family and your boyfriend. If you talk to the police, I will hunt you down for the rest of your life and I *will* kill you."

I felt somewhat amazed that fear had left me. I was still empowered with the strength of Almighty God. As soon as he shut the door, I prayed, "Lord, this will not be in vain. Please protect me now," and I raised my head.

I watched as he trotted toward a car parked a few feet away. He turned and saw me. He raised his arm, pointed the gun at my head and squeezed the trigger, his arm shaking as he pulled with all his might.

As I calmly looked down the barrel of that gun, I wonder what he envisioned at that moment. Was he waiting to hear the muffled sound as the bullet sped down the barrel of the gun straight for me? Did he imagine what the bullet would do as it tore through my head?

What was he feeling when nothing happened? Did he wonder why, after he pressed down with all his might, he could not pull the trigger?

His face crumbled with emotion as he once more pointed the gun at my head, aimed anew and struggled mightily to pull the trigger. But it would not budge.

A sense of peace filled my heart. I laughed inside as I pictured an angel's finger jamming the trigger which kept it from disengaging the sear and kept the hammer from striking the firing pin. The bullet, which he had intended to shatter my head, was immobilized by God. My life had been spared by God's direct intervention and my heart leaped for joy.

His face was a contortion of confusion, fear and anger as he quickly lowered the gun in defeat and raced to his car. Before he could drive away, I memorized his license number.

Chapter 6

TENDER
MERCIES

*"Surround me with your tender mercies so I
may live,
for your law is my delight."*

— PSALM 119:77 (NLT)

I watched his car careen toward the exit, tires screeching as it sped through the lot, dangerously fast and nearly out of control. When I could see his car no more, I raised my swollen and bruised wrists to my mouth and chewed the white medical tape until I could rip my hands free. I found my pants wadded up on the floor of the car, pulled them on and buttoned my torn blouse as best as I could. I took a quick look in the rearview mirror and was startled by who looked back at me. My eyes and face were puffy and streaked with black mascara. The hair that I had spent twenty minutes getting just right a few hours before was a mass of wild tangles. I looked frightful and wanted to cry again. But somewhere deep inside, a firm determined strength bolstered me. This would not be in vain.

I wiped away as much mascara as I could, spat out the frayed medical tape that clung to my teeth, pushed back my hair and grabbed my purse. I eased myself out of the car and headed across the parking lot. My eyes focused on the immediate goal: the Pizza Hut, whose sign at that moment seemed a bright beacon leading me to safety. My fingers rummaged frantically in the bottom of my purse, searching for that dime I had found earlier. I pushed aside gum wrappers and lipstick and rejoiced when my fingers wrapped around the familiar shape. I clutched the dime tightly to my chest, thinking about the telephone call I would have to make. Instead of asking my brother to come and pick me up, I'd now have to explain. What would I tell him? How would I tell him? What could I say to make him understand, make anyone understand?

I pushed open the front door of the Pizza Hut and a hush seemed to ripple through the room, replacing the cheerful chatter that had filled the air only moments before. Every eye seemed to turn to me. Several of the kids who worked there attended my high school. The image of my face in the rearview mirror flashed in my mind. No wonder they were staring. One girl I knew opened her mouth to speak to me, but before she could get out the first word, I darted for the bathroom door. I frantically locked the latch behind me and nearly fell. My body began shaking and I looked down at my wrists and torn clothing. Did this really happen? I've got to get to that phone. I picked myself up and made my way as discreetly as possible across the lobby to the pay phone. My hands were sweating as I picked up the receiver. Please be home, someone please be home.

My mother answered the phone.

"Mama?" was all I could get out before my voice splintered with emotion.

"What's wrong?"

"I—I—I've been attacked."

"Attacked!"

"Mama, I've been raped."

"Oh my baby, oh no! How badly are you hurt?"

"I need someone to come and get me."

"Where are you?"

"I'm at Pizza Hut in the mall parking lot."

"I'll be right there."

I hung up the telephone and turned to see that everyone was staring at me. Many faces looked at me with concern, but I couldn't stand all those probing eyes. I turned around and headed for the bathroom and locked myself inside a stall. It seemed like an eternity before I heard a knock on the stall door. Every joint and muscle ached and my thoughts were blurred. My mind was blank. Time was playing tricks again, stretching out before me into what seemed like hours, then snapping back into minutes again. How long had I been there?

"Leisha, are you sick? Is there anything I can do?" It was Susan, one of my classmates who worked behind the counter.

"I'm okay, thanks. My mom is coming to get me."

"Are you sure?"

"Yes."

"Well . . . Okay, then. Let me know if you need anything."

I heard the door hiss shut as Susan left. It must have been just moments later, but it seemed like hours before I heard the door open again and heard my mama's voice.

"Leisha? Leisha honey, are you in here?"

"Here. Here, Mama, I'm here," I said as I fumbled to unlock the door and fell into her arms.

"Oh, baby, baby," she said as she wrapped her arms around me and hurried me out of the bathroom, past the counter, past all those inquisitive eyes, and out the door.

Joey was waiting outside. I tried to tell them what had happened, but words seemed to get in the way of what was inside my mind. The story came out in bits and pieces and I knew I wasn't making much sense to them.

From where we stood, we could see Mama's car and it was surrounded by policemen. Some had small brushes and were dusting it for fingerprints. Of course, it dawned on me, my family had called the police. I hadn't anticipated that.

Two of the officers left my mama's car and walked toward us.

"Leisha?" the shorter of the two said.

"Yes."

"I'm Detective Brimmer and this is Sergeant Mallory," he said, nodding to his partner. "Mind answering a few questions?"

"Go ahead," I said, although my head began to swim and I felt dizzy. Everything seemed to take forever to be over in a second.

I remember seeing their mouths move. I must have answered them, because they kept moving their mouths. But I don't remember what they asked or what I answered. Their faces were clear, but the edges of the parking lot seemed fuzzy. They walked away from me and I overheard Detective Brimmer say to Joey:

"We'll finish up here and meet you there."

My mind was a blur. I felt strangely numb. I don't remember getting into a car, but my mind snapped alert as we pulled into the parking lot of the hospital emergency room. The sky was black. Where did the daylight go?

We walked inside the hospital and my mama whispered something to someone behind the desk and we were immediately taken to a big room lined with hospital beds. The nurse led me to a bed, pulled the curtain, and she and Mama helped me undress and put on a soft, cotton hospital gown. I eased into bed and closed my eyes, my head now throbbing and my entire body aching.

"We've got an assault case here, did anyone call the police?" I heard someone say outside my drawn curtain. Joey frowned and stepped out to tell the nurses that the detectives were on their way. Soon, Patch and Kenny arrived.

They both rushed over to the hospital bed and I sat up to hug them and reassure them that I was okay. But I could hardly manage to put my arms around them. I felt weak and sick to my stomach and slid from their arms back onto the bed.

I wished a nurse would appear with a needle filled with a strong sedative so I could escape into sleep. I wanted to disappear, dissolve into the sheets. I felt so ashamed. Where was Tom? Did anyone tell him? What was everyone thinking? Their blank looks only left me to guess. No one in my family knew what to say.

The detectives had plenty to say.

"Miss Miller, you need to tell us everything. Why were you shopping? Why did you park so far away? Why did you let him help you? Did you know this man? Why do you think . . . ? "Why?" "Why?" "Why?"

The questions went on forever. I wished I knew the answers. I knew this was important but kept wondering, why all the "whys" about me? What about the whys about the man who lay in wait for an innocent victim, who just happened to be me, by the way, and then violently attacked her? Did they think I enticed him? Did they think I invited this? Oh, how could they? It could have been anyone. What were they thinking? Was this my fault? Oh, what was everyone thinking?

God, I know You saved my life, that Your words stopped a bullet and sent a violent, brutal rapist fleeing in terror of Your might. But how do I convey that to these big, official police officers in their creaking leather and holstered guns who are used to dealing with evil with brute force, chains and jail cells?

These were days before victim's rights advocates and sensitivity training for officers who interview rape victims, and I knew these men were just doing their jobs. But I felt so sad, so tired. I wanted to disappear, to retreat somewhere, anywhere. But there was nowhere to go. Instead, I pulled the thin, white cotton hospital blanket to my chin and slowly answered their questions. All of them. As best I could.

After the policemen left, the business of the emergency room swirled around me as I waited, for quite some time, to see a doctor. The examination was so cold, so fast. The instruments were hard and harsh to my wounded body. There were no reassuring words, no outward signs of compassion, as the doctor checked for broken bones, gave me a pelvic examination, a sedative, and advised me to follow up with my own doctor. Then he was gone.

The drive home seemed like an eternity. Every bump in the road jarred my aching joints, caused my bruises to throb. From way down my street, I could see the lights from our big picture window welcoming me home. Our house had never looked so good. But who did all those cars belong to? Oh no, I didn't think I could face anyone.

I hesitated getting out of the car and Patch walked around to the passenger side, picked me up in his big strong arms and carried me through the front door and into my mother's bedroom. He laid me in the middle of my mom's king-size bed. I looked around the room. Why were all these people here? I realized I was surrounded by the people I loved most in the world.

They were all there, Pastor Weaver, our dear friend Coach Regnier and his wife, Carol, Tom's older brother Marty, Patch, Kenny and Joey, Mama and Tom. Oh, I didn't want to look at Tom's face. I just wanted to curl up into a ball and die. What, God? What will my Tom think of me now? A month before our wedding! O God the hurt in his face. I could hardly bear to look at him. No one said anything. I felt so numb. What was Tom thinking?

No one knew what Tom was thinking.

Tom had been in Detroit at his brother Marty's house when his mother called with the news that I had been raped. Marty began talking in hushed tones, turned his back to Tom and walked away, but his astonished voice was loud enough to carry back to Tom.

"Leisha's been raped?!"

Big, strong Tom, who was always in total control of his emotions and seldom showed signs of weakness, began to cry. Kathy, Marty's wife, ran to Tom, wrapped her arms around him and admonished Marty for being so careless.

Seconds later, Tom and Marty climbed into our new van that moments ago had been such a source of pride. Now Tom just wanted to see how fast it could take him to me. Tom tried to climb into the driver's seat, but Marty saw how upset he was and refused to let him drive. Marty floored the accelerator, and the van shot down the highway at ninety miles an hour, but the questions in Tom's mind flew at him even faster. Where had I been? What had I been doing? How did this happen? Why hadn't he been there to stop it? Why had my mother squandered all the insurance money from my dad's death and had to drive such a broken-down car anyway? Why had he ever let me go shopping alone? Why he had let me out of his sight? Why had I wanted to compete in this pageant anyway? Tom's mind was full of blame, a lot of blame.

Just weeks earlier, Marty had been one of the first officers in the Detroit Police Department to take a new rape training course, which taught how to compassionately and gently deal with victims. Only days before, he had completed the session. As the van raced closer to my house, Marty coached Tom on what to say, how to say it and what I would be feeling. Tom tried to take all the information in, telling himself over and over again to watch what he said, to be very sensitive, to not show how angry he was so I wouldn't misunderstand and think he was blaming me. He wanted to behave godly, despite the emotional torrent that raged inside him.

Flashing red lights from a Michigan State Police trooper's car interrupted Tom's thoughts. Marty pulled off the road and talked to the officer. After the trooper heard the story and saw Marty's badge, he sent them on their way.

It had to be somebody's fault, Tom was thinking. Wasn't he supposed to protect me?

As he walked into my house and joined the others who were waiting for me to come home from the hospital, Tom, the All-American high school and college wrestler, the undefeated state champion, the powerful athlete, the strong and godly man, was overcome with helplessness and hopelessness, which gave way to rage and frustration.

As Patch brought me into the bedroom, Tom even felt angry that he hadn't been the one to carry me into the house. Tom was enraged that my family was so tolerant and forgiving and seemed to passively accept the worst circumstances with little resistance. His thoughts became irrational. The Lebanese blood that flowed in Tom's veins began to boil with outrage and he began to thirst for vengeance.

Tom was thinking about a conversation his brother Marty had with Toledo police officers earlier in the evening. Tom had overheard and remembered it all.

As he stood with others around my bed, no one knew that Tom was thinking about the black 1967 Chevy Impala, four-door, Ohio license A-26898, and of Donald Lee Hollabaugh, twenty-three-year-old Caucasian male, who drove that car. Tom was thinking about the years he had spent building up his body, developing strong, powerful muscles that served him well.

Tom was thinking about murder.

But Tom didn't say a word, and his face never betrayed him to any of us. It was composed, tender even, as he walked over to the bed and wrapped his arms around me. I buried my face in his soft, cotton shirt and cried. Then Marty, God bless him, big, bad, macho Marty, lieutenant on the Detroit police force, quietly knelt down at the foot of the bed, folded his hands and bowed his head to pray. Slowly everyone in the room knelt, bowed their heads and joined him in prayer.

"Dear God," Marty prayed, "be with our precious sister. Comfort her by the Holy Spirit, stand by her and fill her with Your peace."

The love and gratitude for my family overpowered the pain that racked my body and soul. My heart was filled with thanksgiving as tears poured down my cheeks.

I looked around the room at the faces of our loved ones, our families, Tom's and mine, who had gathered there. Their approval of our upcoming wedding had been important to me, but both our families had been against our marrying. I was only eighteen and just weeks out of high school. They thought I was too young and Tom, at twenty-two, was not quite ready for the responsibilities a family would bring.

But here in this moment God answered our prayer. For the first time, our families realized how much Tom and I loved each other. They could see how tenderly we held each other and felt the hurt for each other. In that room, joined in prayer, our families united in love and support.

Later, when we were alone, Tom held me in his arms while I cried bitter tears of regret, pain and mourning for what I had lost, what we both had lost. Although I had been violated by several men in ways no child should ever suffer during my lost childhood, and had yielded to drugs in my misspent youth, I had never given in to teenage sex. I had been a virgin. I had held close to my heart the quiet comfort that I could share that precious moment with Tom on our wedding night. And now that, too, was gone. After a very long time, I was the first to speak.

"Please don't hate me," I whispered, hiding my face in his chest as he held me close.

"I could never hate you," he said softly. "I don't want you to worry, I'm right here with you."

He put a finger beneath my chin, lifted it and cupped my face with both hands.

"Look at me, Leisha, and listen to me. He only touched your body. Don't let him touch your soul. That is the one thing you have control over. He can't ever have that part of you."

Those words were a balm to my heart and I thanked God that in the midst of tragedy, His tender mercies abound.

Chapter 7

WHOM
SHALL
I FEAR?

"The Lord is my light and my salvation;
Whom shall I fear?
The Lord is the strength of my life;
Of whom shall I be afraid?"

— P S A L M   2 7 : 1   (N K J)

Our wedding was one month to the day away as I found myself clinging desperately to Tom's strong arm in the backseat of an unmarked police car as we drove from parking lot to parking lot in search of my rapist's car.

I hadn't slept at all the night before. The sedative the doctor had given me hadn't worked and my mind kept thrusting me into the middle of the rape. Over and over again, I thanked God for saving my life. I marveled at God's sheer power and faithfulness to be with me always. When words failed me, I prayed in my spirit knowing that God would understand my heart. I basked in His presence and tried to rest.

Detective Brimmer's telephone call came early the next morning.

"Because you were so clear-minded in your descriptions and gave us his license number, we think we've located him," he said. "If you're up to it, we'd like you to come down to the station."

I had been stunned. I couldn't remember giving the police the license number.

Tom had driven me downtown to the old gray building and we were led to the basement where Detective Brimmer and his partner, Detective

Foster, were waiting. Detective Brimmer had to clear the wooden chairs of newspapers and files before Tom and I could sit down. On his desk was a half-empty family-size bottle of Pepto-Bismol. Its empty twin was lying on top of crumpled papers that were stuffed in an overfilled wastebasket.

"We think we've found the guy," Detective Brimmer said. "We're going to drive you by some locations and all we want you to do is look around for his car. If you see it, just point it out to us, okay?"

"Okay," I answered.

We drove directly to the Bargain City parking lot that had been blistering bright the day before, but was gray and dull on this cloudy day. This didn't feel like the Fourth of July.

"No, I don't see anything like his car."

We drove across the street to the Greenwood Mall parking lot, passing the movie theater where I'd seen many films as a kid and the dime store where I'd parted with many a week's allowance.

"No, I don't see anything."

"Are you sure? Look again, be sure."

"I'm sure."

We drove several miles and pulled into the parking lot of a Hostess Day Old Bread store. My throat tightened as I recognized his car parked in front of the store. O my God, did that mean he was inside?

"That's it," I said, my voice sounding much stronger than I felt. "I'm sure. That is the car he drove away in."

"All right, that's all we needed," Detective Brimmer said as he slowly drove away. "You've done real well, Leisha."

My stomach churned as Tom drove me home. I was relieved that the police had found him so quickly, but I knew the days to come would bring a horror of their own. Tom looked grim as he leaned over and kissed me good-bye.

"Aren't you going to come in?" I asked.

"No, I have something I have to do."

I stood on the porch and watched him drive away without looking back.

Tom drove directly to his house and walked in without a word.

"Hello, Tommy, how did it go with the police?" Tom's mother asked. But he brushed past her and walked to his bedroom, coming out just moments later.

"Tommy . . ."

"Oh, fine, Mom. Fine. They found him."

"Found him! Wait, where are you going?"

"I have something to do," Tom said, hurrying out the front door.

Tom looked at the sharp blade on the sturdy army knife on the seat beside him as he pushed the gas pedal. It looked threatening and deadly, just like he felt. His heart burned with a need for vengeance. At the speed he was traveling, it didn't take Tom long to reach the Hostess store. He slammed on the brakes, grabbed the knife and burst through the door.

Inside, the bakery workers saw the knife and scattered.

"Who owns that car out there?" Tom shouted, pointing to the vehicle I'd just identified.

The workers, who were hiding behind counters and bread racks, were silent.

"I said I want to know who owns that car because I'm going to kill him," Tom shouted again.

From behind a bread rack a frightened voice said, "You're too late, buddy, the police just picked him up."

Tom shook with fury as he got in his car and drove home.

. . .

When he picked me up the next day to go to the police station again, Tom's face didn't show what he was really feeling and he didn't say a word about what he had nearly done. Detective Brimmer had called and asked us to come to the downtown jailhouse, where a line of prisoners waited for me to pick out the one who had raped me.

I wasn't prepared for what I saw as I walked through the door. The room was filled with somber women and children.

"Detective Brimmer, who are all these women?"

"Victims."

"In other cases?"

"No, Leisha, only one case. This one. Look, we've been onto this guy for a long time. We think he's the same guy who assaulted all these women, but we didn't have enough evidence to link him to anything until you came forward. No one else has been willing to press charges. He told all his victims the same thing: 'I'll hunt you down the rest of your life, I'll kill you, I know where you live.' They're all afraid. Not one has agreed to press charges. We were lucky to get them here today."

I looked into the faces of his victims. Several of them were pretty, young girls, but many were middle-aged and a couple were elderly, including one who leaned heavily on a cane. I assumed the children were there with their mothers.

"Don't you have somewhere for the children to wait while their mothers identify him?" I asked.

"Leisha, those children are his victims, too."

My knees felt weak, and my stomach churned. One little girl couldn't have been more than ten, the other must have been twelve. Who was this monster?

Detective Brimmer stood in the middle of the room and announced: "We're going to lead you into a room one at a time. There will be a two-way glass wall. You'll be on one side and the prisoners will be on the other. They cannot see you, so you needn't be afraid. They have no idea who is identifying them. Take your time and look at each prisoner. If you see the one who assaulted you, identify him by the number above his head."

When my turn came, I was led into a darkened room that was lit by one overhanging bulb. The room on the other side of the glass was well lit. My palms were sweating as I sat down at the table in front of the glass. What if he's not there? What if he's still out there? The prisoners began to fill the room and I noticed that I was holding my breath. I exhaled loudly and began to look for my attacker.

O dear Lord, there he is, number five. I was certain. Something in his eyes triggered the memory of the smell of him, and my nostrils burned with the stench. He was looking straight ahead, not aware of the torrent that was whirling inside me. For one brief second, I wished he could see that I was the one pointing my finger at him. That I was the one with power at that moment, that I held his future in my hands. But I realized that was revenge and certainly not from God and I pushed it away.

"Number five," I said.

"Take your time, Leisha. We want a positive identification. Look at every man up there closely."

"I'm absolutely positive. That's him, number five."

"Okay, take them away," Detective Brimmer said.

"What happens now?" asked Tom.

"Well, we need to see if any of the others will press charges. So far, none of them have been willing."

"Not willing . . . I don't understand," I said.

"Look, Leisha, they're scared to death. Did you see the older woman with the cane? He ran over her with her own van and she will be crippled for the rest of her life. She feels lucky to be alive. This guy is brutal."

A chill ran up my back like icy fingers. Detective Brimmer led us back into the room where the others were waiting. Tom and I sat down and Detective Brimmer told us he'd be right back and left the room.

The room was quiet, no one was talking. I looked at the women around me. I couldn't read their faces, their expressions were blank. Indignation was bubbling inside me and I could contain it no longer.

"How many of you are going to press charges?" I demanded, surprised at the authority in my voice.

My words were met with blank, hard stares. No one responded, and I stood up and faced them. "How can you let him go? How can you let him walk away from what he did to you? Let him go and he'll be free to rape your daughter tomorrow. We have a righteous responsibility here!"

A middle-aged woman looked away. I understood very well what she was feeling. I intimately knew her pain, I burned with the same shame she felt. This was a difficult task before us, fraught with risk and not easy for anyone, yet I knew that it must be done and that we were the ones to do it.

"Well, I'm pressing charges!" I nearly shouted. "I'm cooperating with the police and I'm going to do whatever they need me to do to put this guy away. We have a righteous responsibility to protect other innocent women from him. We are the only ones who know what he is capable of and the job to get him off the streets falls directly on our shoulders. You don't want to get involved? You are already involved. We can't wait for someone else to take care of this, we're the ones who have to do it, don't you understand that? I'd like your help, I'd like all of you to join me. But if I have to do it all alone, I will!"

And I walked out of the room. Tom's eyes grew large. I don't think he knew what to think. He'd never seen me this way, I'd never seen myself this way. Detective Brimmer told all of us to go home and get some rest and that he would call us and let us know the next step. He told us all the women and the little girls had identified the same man and that his name was Donald Hollabaugh.

I fumed all the way home. I was indignant. How could I be the only one willing to do anything? Weren't they angry about what had happened to them? Didn't they want to put him behind bars so other women wouldn't have to suffer the same kind of harm, humiliation and perhaps even murder at his hands? Then my heart softened and I felt pity for them. I was in distress, too. My soul was writhing, too. I reprimanded myself for being so harsh. Where's your heart, Leisha? I demanded of myself. Didn't you see that poor woman on a cane? Didn't you see those little girls?

The next day, Pam Ansted, my friend and the other contestant from our town, and I loaded the van and left for Kalamazoo, Michigan, and the Miss Teen USA pageant. Everyone had tried to talk me out of it, but I had worked too hard to just give up. The first few miles were jovial, as Pam and I talked about the pageant and our anticipation, our recent high school graduation and my upcoming wedding, until the even bigger issue that we had deftly avoided could be ignored no longer.

I sighed with resignation. "Does everyone know?"

Pam smiled softly at me. "No, only a few people are talking about how brave you are and how amazed they are that you are going ahead with the pageant and your wedding. No one knows many details of what happened."

So I told Pam the whole story. Surprisingly I could feel myself getting stronger with each word. When I finished, she was crying. I pulled into a gas station and we were both glad for the reprieve. After I filled the tank and took an icy Pepsi she handed me, I gave Pam a big hug. We piled back in the van and talked only about the pageant for the rest of our journey.

We checked in at the Kalamazoo Hilton, the same hotel that hosted the pageant the previous year, and were assigned roommates.

There were three other girls assigned to my room, and I couldn't wait to meet them. I loved getting to know the other girls and learning about their hometowns, but they weren't there when I dropped off my suitcases. The packet of schedules and events weighed heavy in my hand

My brother Kenny and I, age two, set for Easter.

My daddy, William Roger Miller.

Me, age eight, the year Daddy died.

I'll always be grateful to Jackie and her family for taking me to this church, where I became a Christian.

Recently I reunited with Pastor J. D. Montei, who baptized me!

I was thrilled when in my junior year of high school my artwork was displayed at the Toledo Museum of Art.

This is me in my senior year of high school. I was Snowball Queen! My brother Roger (Patch) did the honors and escorted me.

Three days after my attack, I competed in the Miss Teen USA, Miss Michigan pageant. I gave the speech on patriotism I had been planning.

We were honored when Coach Bill Regnier, his wife Carol, and their children Mike and Lori agreed to be in our wedding.

Tom and I on our wedding day.

A happy, happy day. Alex, our gift, was born.

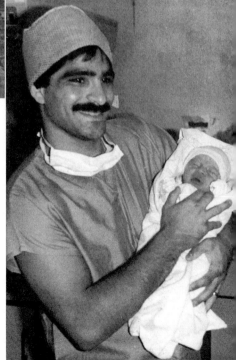

My friend Nicky Cruz, founder and president of Nicky Cruz Outreach.

Bill Biel and Sam Butcher when I worked for Jonathan & David, Inc.

God's general in my life, Dr. James Dobson, founder and president of Focus on the Family.

*Ma Joseph and I
on vacation in
Florida.*

*Tom is still winning wrestling
trophies, now with Alex.*

*My brothers and Mom, Christmas
1997. Left to right, Joe, Kenny, me,
Roger (Patch), and my mom, Elease.*

Alex, Tom, and I today.

and I probably should have sat down to study them, but I couldn't wait to explore that grand hotel. I unpacked quickly and headed straight for the ballrooms, remembering how regal they had seemed to me the year before.

Excitement sizzled like electricity all around me. The lobby was filled with girls who were just arriving and hotel workers who scurried about seeing to the final preparations for the pageant. I felt the familiar strong desire to compete begin to awaken. What a glorious moment.

I stepped on the escalator to go up one floor. I couldn't believe my eyes as I looked at the people approaching on the "down" escalator, opposite me. There he was! He was supposed to be in jail. How could he be here, how could he have known where I was? O God, he was only a few feet away from me, but he hadn't seen me yet. I dropped and crouched beneath the escalator railing, praying he wouldn't see me, my heart thumping loudly. Dear Lord, how did he get out of jail? How did he get here? I clung to my feet, trying to balance myself on the moving stairs until he passed. He was looking the other way as I neared the top. I jumped from the escalator and hid behind a large, leafy plant in a giant planter and watched as he stepped off the escalator.

But wait, this was a different man. It wasn't him at all. What? How could my eyes have deceived me so? Which of that man's features had connected with some lurking memory and persuaded me that he was my attacker? It wasn't him. It wasn't real. The fear that still burned in my veins certainly had been.

I realized that people passing by looked at me cautiously from the corners of downcast eyes. My behavior must have looked strange, I realized. I raced back to my room and burst through the door, not even thinking about my roommates. They were sitting on a bed playing cards. They looked up but I didn't say a word. I bolted for the bathroom. In the mirror I could see mascara dripping down my cheeks. Fortunately I had already placed my Bible in the bathroom, which was my favorite place to study. I loved to read while sitting on the cool tile. I shrank to the floor, hugging my knees to my chest, and began trembling as the tears flowed. I need to get ahold of myself, I reasoned. How else am I going to be able to compete? Oh, what happened to me? I began to pray, O God, I know You were with me in that car, I know You were with me all those times with my mother, I know You were with me when Daddy died, I know You were with me at the police station, I need You now, again, please . . .

My spirit began to calm down and I wiped my face and opened my Bible. Like an old friend, it gave me familiar comfort and strength. My Bible fell open in my lap to Psalm 27:

The Lord is my light and my salvation;
Whom shall I fear?
The Lord is the strength of my life;
Of whom shall I be afraid?
When the wicked came against me
To eat up my flesh,
My enemies and foes,
They stumbled and fell.
Though an army may encamp against me,
My heart shall not fear;
Though war may rise against me,
In this I will be confident.

One thing I have desired of the Lord,
That I will seek:
That I may dwell in the house of the Lord
All the days of my life,
To behold the beauty of the Lord,
And to inquire in His temple.
For in the time of trouble
He shall hide me in His pavilion;

In the secret place of His tabernacle
He shall hide me;
He shall set me high upon a rock.

And now my head shall be lifted up above my enemies all
    around me;
Therefore I will offer sacrifices of joy in His tabernacle;
I will sing, yes, I will sing praises to the Lord.
Hear, O Lord, when I cry with my voice!
Have mercy also upon me, and answer me.
When You said, "Seek My face,"
My heart said to You, "Your face, Lord, I will seek."
Do not hide Your face from me;
Do not turn Your servant away in anger;
You have been my help;
Do not leave me nor forsake me,
O God of my salvation.
When my father and my mother forsake me,
Then the Lord will take care of me.

Teach me Your way, O Lord,
And lead me in a smooth path, because of my enemies.
Do not deliver me to the will of my adversaries;
For false witnesses have risen against me,
And such as breathe out violence.
I would have lost heart, unless I had believed
That I would see the goodness of the Lord
In the land of the living.

Wait on the Lord;
Be of good courage,

And He shall strengthen your heart;
Wait, I say, on the Lord!

I was overcome. Centuries-old words, words that must apply to a million human situations of pain and turmoil, but which my heart knew were just for me, just for that moment. The living, breathing Word of God was speaking to me and empowering me with God's strength. Thank You, God, for Your faithfulness.

That's right, who do I have to be afraid of? What do I have to be afraid of? God jammed that gun. He was with me. He's always been with me and He'll be with me always, just as He promises. He *is* the strength of my life. My enemy did come to eat up my flesh and he stumbled right before my eyes. Confidence and strength, God's strength, were filling me.

I burst open the bathroom door and my roommates looked up, startled. Many girls fall apart in stiff competition and they must have silently put me in that category. I walked out, Bible in hand, and interrupted their card game.

"I must tell you what just happened to me," I began, and I told them the entire story and how God had reached down from heaven and strengthened me in that bathroom.

One of them began to cry. "That happened to me when I was seven and I've never told anyone. It happened in a field on my way home from school."

Another girl, Melanie, said she'd heard of Jesus and that she wanted to invite Him into her life, too. And we prayed together, right there.

I made it through the pageant. I only placed in the top fifteen, but I wasn't disappointed. I knew God had performed several miracles. One of the first telephone calls I received after I returned home was from my pastor, who wanted to see how I was doing.

"Oh, Pastor Weaver, I'm so glad you called," I said. "I need to tell you what happened at the pageant. God's Word is so real and I feel this overwhelming need to tell someone. Can I speak at church? Maybe just at the Sunday night service? I know people are talking and wondering about what happened to me anyway, and maybe it would be best to get it out in the open, and besides, I want them to know what God is doing for me."

Nervously he agreed to allow me to share my story in the Sunday evening service. I was nervous, too. I'd never spoken at church before. I felt highly unqualified, but I knew the things that had happened to me were real and that I could speak with authority.

Sunday morning arrived and Tom and I went to church. I was only a little bit nervous when the pastor announced that I would be speaking that evening. I wanted desperately to look around to judge the reaction of the congregation, but I restrained myself.

The pastor finished the announcements and the words he spoke next seemed to come straight from God just to soothe my heart. "The choir has a special treat for us today. They have a new song, Psalm 27."

Psalm 27!! O God, You're so good. What comfort, what affirmation, You send. I hadn't told anyone except my roommates about Psalm 27. As the choir sang, it seemed as if angels were singing just to me. I cried all the way through the song. Only God and I knew how very much those words meant to me that day.

I arrived for the evening service very early to pray. My mind raced and my body began to sweat. What am I doing? What will I say? Lord, how did I get here anyway? How quickly I had forgotten how God had bolstered me just hours earlier. God must have been frustrated with me, but instead of criticism, Psalm 81:10 came to my mind: "I am the Lord your God, Who brought you out of the land of Egypt; Open your mouth wide, and I will fill it."

Oh, I see, God, we're winging it, I began to pray. Well, I'm glad it's You I'm winging it with. I wouldn't trust anyone else. I missed the remainder of the service because I was entangled in dialogue with God.

True to His promise, as I began to speak, the words poured forth.

As I shared my story directly from my heart, many women pulled tissues from their purses and buried their faces in them. Others were openly crying. When I finished, there was absolute silence. I don't think anyone knew what to do next. Several women got out of the pews and walked to the altar. One woman threw herself on the altar and began to sob. I looked at the pastor questioningly and he nodded. I made my way down the stairs to the altar, where numerous others were kneeling and crying. I could feel their pain, their tears. I put my arm around each one and sobbed with them.

"That happened to me when I was a little girl and I've never told anyone," one said.

"I'm a visitor, I've never been to this church, but I just felt compelled to come tonight. Now I know why," an elderly lady shared. "That happened to me, too."

I prayed with each person. When it was over, I was exhausted, but it was a good tired. I looked up to heaven, and in my heart I could feel God smiling. What a wonder to be able to share God's blessings in such a personal way, to be able to say, "I know what you're feeling, I've been there, and just let me tell you what God did for me. Have you ever read His Word, this passage?"

My heart was telling me that this evening marked the beginning of something new inside me: a burning desire to bring healing to others; to help mend broken people; to simply share and watch God work in their hearts. I felt thrilled that I could be used in such a way and I knew it was what God wanted me to do.

After that night, invitations to speak began to flow. The first came from a women's group. One of their members had heard me at the church. Then someone who had been at the women's group recommended me to a doctors' group, and the requests kept coming.

In mid-July, Detective Brimmer called to tell me that a date for Hollabaugh's pretrial hearing had been scheduled and it was only days away.

"Are you ready, Leisha?"

Was I ready? I was in the middle of planning my August 4 wedding. But it was clear that I had to be ready.

Tom and I met the detectives in the courthouse and they took us to an unoccupied office down the hall to talk.

"Leisha, the good news is you won't be alone. One other woman has agreed to testify with you, but you're going first. You need to tell every detail you remember, it's important that the judge hear everything. But we do have one concern. We don't want anyone to think you had feelings for this guy, so when it comes to that part where you talk about that love stuff, unless you're specifically asked, can you skim over that part?"

"I have to tell the truth."

"Oh, of course. Please don't misunderstand. We're not asking you to lie. Not at all. We need you to tell everything, but we just don't want anyone to get the wrong idea, so choose your words carefully, and if you can, move quickly over that part."

I understood their point, but I also knew those were the very words that saved my life. Those were the very words that made him tremble. I went into the bathroom and prayed, God, I understand their concern. If anyone believes I had feelings for him they could throw this out of court. But God, I also know You gave me those words. I wouldn't have said them under my own strength. You saved my life with those words. Wouldn't an omission be a lie?

Psalm 119:43–46 came into my mind: "Take not the word of truth utterly out of my mouth, for I have hoped in Your ordinances. So shall I keep Your law continually, forever and ever. And I will walk at liberty, for I seek Your precepts. I will speak of Your testimonies also before kings, and will not be ashamed."

I had my answer. I couldn't be ashamed of what God had done for me. Psalm 7:10 came to me as a punctuation point behind the answer: "My defense is of God, who saves the upright in heart."

Tom and I sat with Detective Brimmer in the courtroom. People around us talked quietly as we all waited for the attorneys and the judge to finish their conference. From where I sat, I could see Hollabaugh, at his place at the defense table. He presented himself to the court in a conservative blue suit and tie, his hair recently cut and neatly combed, hands folded in his lap. To all who cast eyes his way, he looked the perfect gentleman. As I stared at the back of his head, he slowly turned. His eyes found Tom and me, and his calm, cool expression twisted into a sinister grimace, menacing and full of hate.

Tom leaped from his chair and lunged toward Hollabaugh, but Detective Brimmer grabbed his arm and pushed him back into his seat.

"Don't do it, Tom," he said. "You will be thrown right out of this courtroom and Leisha needs you here. Don't do it."

Reluctantly Tom sat down, but his breathing was still labored as he grabbed my hand. I began to pray that God would calm his spirit and give him the strength to go through the trial. Hollabaugh seemed to enjoy Tom's open display of anger. He turned again and scowled at me, his eyes full of malice. I hated the sight of him and I hated what I would have to do: tell the world what had happened in the backseat of my mother's car. I hadn't even shared some of the details with Tom and I feared how he would take hearing it.

The judge called the first witness. That was me and I felt a chill run up my back as I passed Hollabaugh on my way to the witness box. He was only twelve short feet away. He glared at me again, his eyes narrowing into those familiar slits. I looked away.

"Leisha, what happened on July 3, 1979?"

My mind scurried with answers. What happened? I've asked myself that a million times over and over. What did I do? Was it because I had blond hair? I'm not really sure about any of that, but I am sure what God did that day and I silently asked Him to help me organize my thoughts as I answered. I calmly described every detail of the assault and I could almost sense the prosecutor and the police detectives collectively holding their breaths as I came to the "love" part, the part that many of them could not understand. But I was not afraid, I was not nervous or timid.

"He put the gun to my head and told me to shut up, to stop praying or he would blow me into a million pieces." I paused and I looked Hollabaugh right in the eye. And I said with all the conviction and courage and strength that God was pouring through my veins at that moment, "And I said, 'Go ahead and every piece will love you.'"

Hollabaugh looked startled. He dropped his head into his hands. He began to sob and beat the table with his fists. The beating rang loudly in my ears like a drum of victory. A police officer grabbed my arm and escorted me from the courtroom, which had suddenly become a flurry of activity. Lawyers were jumping to their feet, demanding the judge's attention. What was happening? I felt Tom's reassuring arm around me and soon Detective Brimmer came through the double swinging doors.

"After your testimony he confessed to everything! We got him! You did real good, Leisha. You did real good."

I was too stunned to answer. A tall, distinguished man walked quickly from the courtroom, looking distraught.

"Who is that?" I asked.

"That's his brother and that woman with the little girl, they are his wife and daughter, and that gray-haired lady is his mother. They're in more pain than you can imagine. They had no idea."

I looked at his wife. She was beautiful. Her long hair fell attractively over her petite shoulders, and what about his little girl, his innocent little girl? Oh, my fingers deadened with disbelief. I felt so torn for them.

Hollabaugh had faced eight counts ranging from rape to kidnapping to attempted murder. He plea-bargained the charges down to two counts of rape and received two consecutive four-to-twenty-five-year sentences for each count.

"You can go on and be married without a worry," said Detective Brimmer. "He's going away for a long time thanks to you. I wish you the best in everything, Leisha."

That's what I thought, too, that day in the courthouse with Tom's strong arm around me. Finally I could get on with my life. I could be married and close this chapter forever. I watched as police officers pulled Hollabaugh's hands behind him and clanked the handcuffs shut. Before the police officers escorted him away, Hollabaugh turned and gave me one more dark and foreboding look. The message he intended to convey needed no words.

Hollabaugh was still looking back at me when police officers walked him out of the courthouse and into the tunnel system that connected with the Lucas County Jail. What happened during that brief walk caused the investigating officer to file the following report, which was attached to Hollabaugh's permanent record.

Hollabaugh had been very upset, the officer wrote. He kept saying the woman who had testified against him was lying and that he had never seen her in his life.

Hollabaugh asked the officer if he could have a cigarette and was given one as they kept walking. About halfway through the tunnel, Hollabaugh calmed down, turned to the officer and said, "Do you know that St. Charles has a psychiatric ward?"

I told him I did know that, the officer wrote. Then Hollabaugh said, "I told my attorney that I had just left there and that I didn't know what I was doing when I raped the first two."

Chapter 8

ASHES
INTO GOLD

*"To all who mourn in Israel, he will give
beauty for ashes, joy instead of mourning,
praise instead of despair."*

— ISAIAH 61:3 (NLT)

Our small town was so close-knit that the postmistress telephoned me when the wedding dress I had ordered from a large bridal salon in the city arrived at the post office. She and the other women postal workers were as excited as I was and strongly hinted that I drive down there and open the box so they could see the dress.

But I told them they had to wait, just like everyone else in town, and to tell the postman to bring it with the regular mail.

"And I'll know if you've peeked," I teased.

The wedding was a little over a week away, and there were so many details yet undone. Unlike most brides who plan large weddings, I didn't have the luxury of time. I found a willing helpmate in Mama, who was extremely pleased to prepare a guest list and help me select flowers.

Ours was to be a rainbow-theme wedding. Each bridesmaid wore a different-colored pastel dress, so Mama and I chose carnations and daisies that could be tinted to match.

The last task on my long checklist was a trip to the doctor. Ma Joseph agreed to accompany me to his office for the blood test I would need for the marriage license, and the post-rape follow-up examination the doctor would perform at the same time.

I expected nothing unusual. I had suffered some tearing in the rape, but was healing as expected, and the tests for diseases had come back negative, thank God.

But the doctor took much longer than I expected as he performed the pelvic examination. When he finished, he took a long time washing his hands before he spoke to me.

"Um . . . your uterus seems to be inflamed," he said, frowning. "But it's too early to tell about anything and I don't want you to worry."

"What do you mean?" I asked.

"Well, honey, your uterus is inflamed and slightly enlarged, but if there is a problem, we can take care of it. Just don't worry, it's too early to tell."

"What kind of problem? Do you mean he gave me some kind of disease? Is it serious?" I was becoming alarmed.

"Well . . . I don't want to talk about it until we're sure. But we'll take care of it."

One look at Ma Joseph's crumbling face, and I knew. Pregnant! They feared I might be pregnant from the rape. O Lord, Heavenly Father, haven't I suffered enough? I began to pray. Then I realized "the problem" the doctor was referring to was a baby. Did "we'll take care of it" mean abortion? Lord God, I began to pray, I know my life is a gift from You and so is this baby's, however he came into the world. Though my body began to tremble, I prayed, God, I will accept whatever is ahead of me, and I will trust You to see me through this, too.

"We need to perform some tests," the doctor began.

But I interrupted him. "Not now, I'm sorry, I can't do this now. I just want to go home."

All the way home, my heart raced as I thought about having to tell this latest news to Tom, a brand-new Christian who was just learning that following Jesus Christ didn't make you exempt from life's troubles. What would he do? What would he say? He will probably leave me, I thought to myself. I'd better be prepared for that.

I had told Tom I needed to talk to him about something very important and he had rushed over. As he held my hand sitting next to me on the couch, I had a difficult time beginning; the lump in my throat made it hard for me to talk.

"Tom, the doctor says my uterus is enlarged, and that means I might be pregnant," I said, and started to cry. I searched his face for signs of anger or feelings of betrayal but found only compassion. I collapsed in Tom's arms and cried for a long time as he stroked my hair.

"I won't blame you if you want to back out of the wedding," I finally brought myself to say, still sobbing.

"What? Back out! Is that what you've been thinking? How could you think that, Leisha? I love you. What kind of man do you think you're marrying anyway? We'll face this together, the way we'll face all our problems in life, and we'll begin by praying."

Tom took my hand and began to pray for me, for us, for God's will to be done in our lives, and I immediately began to hemorrhage. I bled heavily for nine days. We never knew if I had been pregnant or not. I had rushed from the doctor's office before he could perform any tests. But if I had been pregnant, the doctor said I had miscarried. A "spontaneous abortion" is what he called it.

I was determined not to let anything spoil my wedding day. The daisies and carnations I carried in my bouquet provided the only splash of color against my snow-white dress with the dainty cap sleeves, delicate lace bodice and a floor-length, flowing organza skirt.

The church was filled with our families and dear friends. Carol and Coach Regnier had agreed to stand up for us, and their daughter Lori was our flower girl. I selected as my maid of honor the person who was responsible for bringing Tom and me together in the first place, Mary, my dear friend and Tom's little sister. Amid the happy commotion, Mama grabbed my hand and somehow we found an empty room where we could be alone while I pinned on her corsage.

"There you are, Mama. You look so pretty."

"And you, Leisha. You're more beautiful than I could have imagined," she said with tears in her eyes. Then she smiled weakly and grasped my hand between hers. Her whole body was shaking. She opened her mouth to speak and struggled for words, the tears openly flowing.

"Leisha . . . I . . . I . . ."

"It's okay, Mama. It's okay."

"No, Leisha, it's not okay."

I put my arms around her.

"Oh, Leisha, I want so much for your life to be better. I feel so guilty about everything."

"Mom, please, you don't have to do this. I just want you to enjoy this day with me. I want you to be happy today."

"I am happy, darling. I just love you so much and I don't know how to tell you how very sorry I am."

"I know, Mama."

"Well, then," she said, nodding her head, her lips pressed together in a firm line. "Well, then . . ."

Mama smiled weakly at me and paused for a few moments before beginning again. "Honey, we have a saying in the South where I grew up. When you get married you're supposed to have something old, something new, something borrowed, something blue. Here's the something old. Please accept it as a gift from me and your dad."

Into my hand she placed the engagement and wedding rings that she had worn when she married my father.

"I hope you will always keep these."

"Oh, Mama, I will," I said, and I slipped them on my right hand. The fit was perfect. "Thank you."

Then she handed me an envelope. "Read this later, sweetheart."

I tucked the envelope into my purse, and we walked arm in arm into the vestibule. Mama took her seat in the church and I took Patch's arm. The night before, I had asked Patch for his blessing; his approval meant a great deal to me. "Of course you have my blessing," he had said. "All I ever wanted was your happiness, Leisha."

As we stood in the doorway, awaiting our musical cue, Patch squeezed my hand and smiled encouragingly at me.

My dress shimmered in the candlelight as my brother walked me down the aisle. I glanced at the people in the pews as we walked, but my eyes were drawn to the man who would be my husband. As he waited for me at the altar, Tom's eyes, soft with love, matched my own.

We had a beautiful wedding. The church choir performed several of our favorite songs and Pastor Weaver sang a song he had written about the deep love between the biblical friends Jonathan and David, the King of Israel. Their story had always held a special meaning for me. The special bond they shared was pure and centered in God. They understood each other and knew so well each other's hearts and intents. And this was my hope for our marriage. The first time I ever saw Tom cry was when our pastor sang the words he had written especially for us:

> David, in you I see the love of God.
> I feel a kindred spirit much deeper than blood.
> I sense a loyal heart and on you I can depend.
> Let's join our hearts in covenant, my friend.
> I care about everything you do
> And my heart is united with you.
> With God as our father
> We'll see each other through.
> My brother, my friend, I love you.

It was a good thing we planned our buffet reception in the high school gymnasium. We needed the space. We had invited only three hundred people, but five hundred showed up, and we were happy to have them. After dinner, everyone danced to music performed by the Christian band we'd hired from our church, and to Lebanese music performed by the many talented musicians in Tom's family. When the "Wedding Celebration Song" was played, Tom's family taught the traditional Arab wedding line dance to everyone who wanted to learn. It was a joyous celebration.

Much later that night I pulled Mama's letter from my purse and was touched by her sweet words and the meaning behind them. She wrote:

> *Dearest Leisha,*
> *There are many things in my heart that are left unsaid,*
> *So I'm going to write them on paper instead.*
> *As you walk away, don't ever look back.*
> *The sad times are over and all is intact.*
> *God gave you to me, a prized package of gold*
> *And through your way of living, He did a portrait unfold.*
> *As you travel life's pathways, continue your work,*
> *Remember your husband, and him do not shirk.*
> *Life is a struggle from starting to end,*
> *So when the going gets tough, remember your friend.*
> > *Love, Mom*

She added her telephone number and a Scripture reference, Psalm 23:4: "Yea, though I walk through the valley of the shadow of death, I will fear no evil: for thou art with me; thy rod and thy staff they comfort me."

Perhaps some would think it a strange verse for a wedding, but Mama knew something of the pain born of unfulfilled expectations and splintered dreams. I soon learned that the verse was appropriate for me, too. Sometimes I felt as if I were facing the death of my dreams and all I had hoped for. While Tom and I began our life together full of love, and with all the appropriate aspirations, after one short week we clearly saw that we both had brought heavy baggage into the marriage, but that mine was bigger. Much bigger. What we didn't know was that we were on a collision course with disaster.

Each time Tom touched me, I'd pull away, my emotions shutting themselves down one by one. No one was more surprised than I. What was wrong with me? These were the days I'd waited for all my life. Now was the time to celebrate and enjoy each other, but I just couldn't. I was ashamed. Here was the man of my dreams and I couldn't even respond to him. He deserved better than this. Tom was extremely patient and tried to be kind, but neither of us understood what was happening.

I thought I had the perfect plan for our marriage. I would escape the chaos of my home and create my own environment with my love, one free of pain and abuse. Surely I can be happy now, I pleaded to God. Surely my life can begin now. But that wasn't happening. Why? And why couldn't I respond to this man I loved?

Tom was dealing with issues of his own. Too often he would reach inside one of his emotional bags and pull out anger. He could be abrupt with his words and cut my heart in two with his cruelty. There were times I honestly asked God if I'd heard Him right, if this was truly the man for me. Once at a restaurant, he became angry over something and he frightened me. I told him I wanted to go home. When he didn't respond, I left to telephone for a ride, but before I could dial, Tom burst into the phone booth.

"I'll take you home," he shouted, grabbing my arm and forcing me into the car. He didn't say a word all the way home. I sat quietly, confused and hurt, praying to God for understanding. Once home, I ran to the bedroom and sobbed.

But I couldn't deal with Tom's anger, because I had my own to contend with. Often, normal disagreements turned into major eruptions. I remember during a planned shopping trip, I ran into a sale. I found a beautiful silk blouse that fit me perfectly for $19.99. I was so excited as I bought it. On our budget I couldn't hope to buy anything that beautiful at its regular price. I knew I'd made a good choice and came home laden with shopping bags, eager to share my good fortune with Tom. But he quickly opened his bag of childhood-poverty issues and I found myself in a heated argument trying to justify the purchase. Tom had grown up very poor. His family had depended on welfare for years and he was determined that would never happen to him. His way of making sure of that was to be very careful with money. I, on the other hand, wanted our life to be wonderful and often overspent our budget trying to achieve perfection.

The more I justified buying the blouse, the angrier Tom became, until our loud words became shouts and Tom started knocking things around. I retreated to our bedroom with my head burning and my temples pulsing wildly. I was crying uncontrollably and found myself furiously beating the wall with my fists. Each whack was harder than the last and I was startled out of my daze of fury when my fist burst through the wall.

I sank to the floor exhausted, and stared at the huge, gaping hole in the drywall, astonished at what I was capable of doing. Tom ran up the stairs and took one look at the wall and another at me on the floor. He was as bewildered as I was. He picked me up and held me in his arms until I stopped crying.

The next morning the sunlight streamed through our window and shone directly on that hole. It was the first thing I saw. What had come over me? What had happened to me? I was suddenly frightened of myself. The flood of anger that poured from me was disproportionate to the disagreement we'd had. I felt I could have killed someone that night.

I had often experienced displaced anger. Some minor disagreement or incident would set me off into a rage. The amount of venomous emotion that would pour from me would scare me. Tom usually bore the brunt of my ire. Sometimes I would be so angry I would fly at him and hit his arms, his chest, with my clenched fists: he would stand there, like a rock or like some unfeeling statue and let me pummel him until my overwhelming emotion was spent. Then, as I cried, he would hold me and comfort me.

This became the pattern of our life as we moved around the country during the early years of our marriage. Tom had injured his back wrestling in college and had dropped out after the coach threatened to pull his scholarship if he didn't continue competing with the use of steroids and Novocain. Using this combination could have resulted in severe permanent injury, as steroids can cause the athlete to feel like working out more often and more vigorously, and the painkiller Novocain would prevent him from knowing when to quit. After prayer, Tom decided he couldn't do that, and we moved to Phoenix, Arizona, where Tom found construction work and I landed a job with a modeling agency.

After his injuries had healed, Tom received another wrestling scholarship, this time at Grand Valley State Colleges in Grand Rapids, Michigan. We moved there and I used my college scholarship to attend the Kendall School of Design, where I studied art and worked part-time at a bank. That's where I met Sam Butcher and Bill Biel of Jonathan & David, Inc., who created Precious Moments keepsakes. They would come to the bank and wait in my long line, often ignoring tellers who weren't busy. We always bantered back and forth.

"When are you going to come and work for us?" Sam would ask.

"We sure could use you," Bill would agree.

I thought they were teasing. But one day a bank executive who was also a Christian pulled me aside, told me who Sam and Bill were and the products they created. "You should see if they are serious," she suggested.

So on my lunch hour, I drove to their business. I was filling out an application when Sam walked in. He took one look at me, laughed, and grabbed the application and tore it up. "You don't have to apply," he said. "You're hired!"

I began by taking telephone orders, worked my way to office manager, where I handled all the licensing, then became the manager of the sales staff. After Sam learned I had a background in art, I was moved into the products division, where Sam consulted me on new products, original artwork, and gave me the responsibility of final approval for the greeting card line. The experience was rich and I loved working for them, but after Tom received his certification in cardiac rehabilitation, we moved to Toledo, Ohio, and Tom went to work at St. Vincent's Hospital. I opened up my own gift shop and began to conduct seminars for corporations and individuals on image and color analysis.

Through all our travels, Tom and I had faithfully read the Bible and were growing as Christians. Tom kept feeling a persistent tug to go into ministry work. He began a yearlong internship at our church, in which he studied and worked under the direction of our pastor. On the weekends, he began evangelistic work by presenting to churches in the area a seminar he had developed on the effects on youth of rock music, drugs and sex.

But clinging to God and each other didn't make our problems go away. All our emotional baggage sat in the corner of our married life, just waiting to be opened again. And we opened them often.

For years I struggled with responding appropriately to my husband's loving touch. Some nights I tried so hard. One night I took a long, relaxing bath, put on one of Tom's favorite nightgowns and opened our bedroom window to let in the warm, fragrant night air. Our only light was the pale moonlight that shone through our window and onto Tom's muscular body. As I looked at him lovingly, I felt very blessed. I marveled at the precious gift God had given to us in a physical relationship that was pure in Him. As Tom approached me, the moonlight hit his chest and something about the shape of it, the position of it, sent my mind reeling. The room began to spin and I detached from where I was. Suddenly I was in the backseat of that green Fury. Horrible memories battered me like blows and I doubled over in intense pain. I clutched my stomach and curled into a writhing ball, and Tom rushed me to the emergency room. After many tests and examinations, doctors sent me home with a clean bill of health. Tom prayed with me and held me through the night.

We were trying to be gentle with each other, but we couldn't begin to understand the underlying forces that motivated our behavior, and we seemed to keep having the same difficulties and arguments over and over again. The only difference was what ignited them.

The cycle came to an end the day I overspent our grocery budget by ten dollars. It was such a small amount, but to us back then, it was catastrophic and I knew Tom would be angry. I sat in the car in front of our small apartment building sobbing for several hours, afraid to go inside. When I finally got the nerve to go in and confess, Tom was furious. He yelled and banged the kitchen chairs and began waving those strong arms around. Though he never touched me, I was traumatized, relating his actions to all the abuse I'd suffered in my life. That night was different from other times we'd argued. He had frightened me so badly I couldn't sleep. The next day when he left for work I was still shaking. God, I can't do this, I said, and pulled "retreat" from my emotional baggage. At that moment, in my frantic state of mind, it seemed the only logical option.

I packed my suitcase, took off my wedding rings and laid them on Tom's dresser. I drove to the bank and withdrew several hundred dollars and drove directly to the bus station, where I bought a ticket for Phoenix. I had loved Phoenix and knew I could get a good job there.

I sat in the bus station, frozen, my clenched fist clutching my one-way ticket. Another familiar defense had returned: I had turned the pain into numbness. I wasn't feeling anything. My tense face must have showed the signs of repressed pain, because the man who had sold me my ticket looked concerned and kept glancing my way. I watched him close his window and walk toward me. He was an older gentleman, and kindly. He must be someone's grandfather, I thought.

"Honey, something wrong? Phoenix is a long way to go by your-self."

As soon as he spoke, I began to cry. "Yeah, well . . ." was all I could get out.

He walked to the counter, picked up a broom and began sweeping around my feet.

"That your car?"

"Yeah, well, it's my husband's now," I said.

"You know you can't just leave that car there, it'll get towed away."

All I could think of was how angry Tom would be at that. "Well, I don't really care what happens to the car."

"I know you don't, but you could be ticketed."

I thought for a moment. "If I give you a number, would you call my husband after I'm gone so he can come and get it?"

"Sure, honey. I'd be glad to."

I found a pen and an old receipt in my purse and scribbled Tom's work number on it. Minutes later, I was stepping on the bus. This felt like a bad dream. How did I get in this situation? The roar of the bus reverberated in my ears and my forehead began to grow numb from resting it against the glass window, but I didn't care. The bus stopped at some small town and the driver suggested everyone get off for a short break. But I didn't move, I sat frozen in my thoughts. What had gone wrong? Why is my life always like a bad dream, Lord? Will it ever get better? I barely noticed the movement around me as everyone piled back on the bus and the roaring engine and the hum of the tires on the road resumed. We stopped twice more, and each time I remained in my seat, staring through the window but not really seeing anything, as my troubled thoughts coiled around each other.

"Leisha!" A familiar voice yanked me from oblivion.

Startled, I looked up to see Tom and Nancy Rupli, a dear friend from church, racing down the bus aisle toward me. For a moment everything was surreal and I thought I was hallucinating. I felt dizzy as Tom grabbed my arm and lifted me from the seat and led me down the aisle and off the bus.

"Wait, I don't want to go with you!" I protested, wrestling free of his grasp. Tom and Nancy followed me back to my seat on the bus.

"I know you don't, but I love you and I want you to come home," Tom said.

I was surprised by the softness in his voice. Nancy, too, looked at me with tenderness and compassion.

"C'mon, Leisha, we're going to take you home," she said.

Before I could respond the bus driver came back.

"Hey, what are you two doing on this bus?" he demanded. He was angry and his firmness startled me. I got up out of my seat and Tom led me down the aisle.

The kind old man at the bus station had called Tom immediately. Tom had raced home and phoned our church looking for our pastor, but Nancy had answered. She had been at church working on a project. Tom and I had long admired Nancy and her husband for their sincerity, fortitude and genuine love for God. I'd always hoped that Tom and I could be like them one day.

Nancy sped to our apartment, picked up Tom, and they traced the bus route, just missing the bus by minutes in two towns. At the third stop, they found me.

That night I felt defeated as I walked through the door of our small apartment.

"I want you to just get some rest," Tom said as he tucked me into bed.

I awakened to the doorbell. It was Pastor Weaver, who had baptized Tom, married us and had been my pastor since I was a teenager. I walked out of the bedroom to greet him, and the concerned look on his face frightened me. I assumed I was in for the lecture of my life. Tom and I gingerly sat on the couch and waited his counsel, silent.

Finally Tom began. "Pastor, I don't know what's wrong with her."

To my surprise, Pastor Weaver, who was generally pretty gentle, spoke up with an authoritative voice. "Wait a minute, Tom. What Leisha did was wrong, yes. But she's not the problem here. You are." And he pointed his finger right at Tom. "She's only responding to you. You're not being sensitive and meeting her needs."

I froze. I didn't know what Tom would do. To my great surprise, he agreed. Soon we were praying and Pastor Weaver was leaving. I was afraid to be alone with Tom, still apprehensive of what might happen. I sealed myself in the bathroom and took the longest shower in history.

When I knew I could delay no longer, I stepped from the bathroom in my bathrobe, dabbing my wet and tangled hair. Through the thick steam, I could smell pizza, my favorite aroma, wafting through the apartment. The smell lured me to the living room, where Tom had spread a tablecloth on the floor. A fire softly crackled in our fireplace, and a candle, the only one we had at the time, was lit. In the center of the cloth was an extra-large pizza and chilled Pepsi. Pizza and Pepsi, unbelievable! My favorite meal in all the world and on the floor in front of a fire! My heart melted and I began to sob. Tom embraced me and gently pulled my left hand toward him and placed my wedding rings back where they belonged. He led me to our picnic on the floor and we began laughing uncontrollably.

We realized many things as we talked deep into the night, most importantly that we had a lot of work to do, individually and together. Tom apologized for being so rigid. His splurging on pizza and Pepsi was the proof I needed that he was sincere. I apologized that my life left me lacking in so many emotional areas. I realized that my overspending was a result of trying to measure up, trying to fulfill an unmet need, trying too hard to have it all. I had been determined my life would never be like it was when I was growing up, but instead of depending on God, I was taking matters into my own hands. I realized that I needed to relinquish control of quite a few things and give them over to God. With Tom's help and more sensitivity training with Pastor Weaver, we were at least on the right road.

Tom became interested in counseling. He began to read books, attended counseling seminars, spoke to pastors and listened to radio programs, all with a goal of helping me. We learned a lot together.

I had thought that I could just go on with my life after the rape, but I began to realize how damaged I had been in my early life. And how deeply I had buried my pain. I was totally unaware of all the hurt that I had bottled up inside. I needed to deal with the feeling that I'd been cheated. I needed to stand up and say, what happened to me, it wasn't right and I'm mad about it! I needed to connect the crime to the punishment. I was also beginning to realize that I didn't know how to have a normal relationship with anyone, let alone a normal man. I had been living in deep denial.

Our bodies and minds respond to psychological pain just as they would to actual physical injury. Our natural instinct is to suppress it, hide it, pretend it didn't happen. We want to believe that if we deny it long enough, it will go away. It doesn't work that way. Beneath the surface, that pain is still seething and someday, some way, it will come out, either publicly or privately. Like a festering splinter, it will push its way through the surface and emerge, often with a different face. Sometimes it will show up as overeating, or overspending, but more often than not it is a destructive force that begins affecting lives, relationships, jobs, finances, and the quality of life is diminished.

The worst and most frightening is anger. A person can lose control, not even know what he is doing, and be helpless to stop. Like most victims, I believed I had it under control. I believed I could just go on with my life and forget the past. But anger is so vile and ugly and it never forgets. It stirs up torment at every opportunity. Anger says, somebody owes me, somebody's going to pay for all the wrong done to me, and it doesn't matter who. Anger says, I will be in control. Anger loves the word "never." Never, never, never again will that happen to me, it says, and I will make sure of it at any price. But anger isn't very smart and never measures the cost of its actions. Anger is the most destructive and strongest force I've ever contended with.

I also learned that I have an incredible ability to never unleash in public. I keep it all under control and save my acrimony for private situations. Unfortunately my husband bore the brunt of the private recriminations and was often shocked by my behavior.

I've often asked him, "Why didn't you leave me? I would have left me." But I know he stayed because of his commitment to God. And I believe God gave him extra measures of grace, in all new shades, to withstand me. God was a participant even in the darkest of times, and He waited until I had someone strong in my life to help me before He showed me the places I needed to heal. And God graciously opened the door to my healing slowly, taking one issue at a time. If He had cleaned house all at once, it would have killed me.

God's Word is the key that will open the locked and secret places where we try to hide the pain from our trauma. The Word of God cleanses, sweeps clean the mess, washes away the pain and shines the light of His Word where there once was darkness. Once He has released us from these strongholds, He will reclaim the area and create a new foundation on which to build. Old patterns are replaced by new ways of thinking, all anchored in God's Word. This makes us ready for the final stage: using everything, our entire lives, for God's glory. Tom and I took comfort in Romans 12:2: "Do not conform any longer to the pattern of this world, but be transformed by the renewing of your mind. Then you will be able to test and approve what God's will is—his good, pleasing and perfect will."

We began to understand who we were in Jesus Christ, not who we were in our own eyes or in the eyes of others. I clearly saw that I was *not* a victim. As the daughter of God, the King of the universe, I truly was a princess.

Chapter 9

REJUVENATION

*"He saved us, not because of righteous
things we had done, but because of his
mercy."*

— TITUS 3:5 (NIV)

Each time I'd read a newspaper story about a rape, or whenever something as benign as the smell of first-aid tape sent me reeling into the backseat of that Fury, I would pray for Hollabaugh: Rejuvenate him, Lord. Open his seared conscience. Let him know his depravity. Let him fall on his face before You and know that You are God.

For that is the only hope any of us have, really, and that is especially true for people like Hollabaugh. Rehabilitation may work for a season, but what is there to sustain it? Without the renewing of our mind in conjunction with the rejuvenation of our spirit in God, there is no rehabilitation, no lasting change.

Nearly every day I prayed that prayer because so often a smell, a color, a sound, a movement, a position of someone's body, would spark horrible memories. In an effort to help me, Tom had been studying Christian counseling as well as the Bible to learn about God's power in the healing process. He assured me that flashback memories were common in rape victims. Some ordinary everyday event could trigger a memory, and the victim would be overcome with terror and helplessness once more, such as I had experienced on the hotel escalator. This revelation enlightened me and gave me comfort that my reactions weren't crazy.

Tom counseled me further that God hasn't given us the spirit of fear, but rather the power of love and a sound mind. A physical injury inflicted by an enemy will eventually heal. But fear or bitterness that isn't dealt with could keep a victim bound and eventually destroy her. Consider the biblical example of Tamar, who was raped by her half brother Amnon. Her brother Absalom told her to "keep silent" and she remained "desolate" in his house.

I looked up the word "desolate" in the thesaurus and read its companion words: barren, devastated, deprived, destitute, deserted, lonely, friendless, hopeless, forlorn, dreary, dismal, gloomy, saddened, forsaken, abandoned, ruined, sorrowed, grieved, woeful and given up. That sounded just like me. I had been, in different times in my life, intimately acquainted with each one.

Fear wasn't an issue with me anymore. God had removed that from my heart with Psalm 27 while I lay crumpled on the hotel bathroom floor. As I struggled to overcome the other painful legacies of my past, I clung to the promise that there is victory in Jesus Christ. God wants us to live in faith. And with Him, there are no dead-end streets: anyone can be healed.

Tom had begun working in the behavioral medicine field in an adolescent treatment unit, and some of the situations he observed hit home. At times, he felt he was looking into a mirror when he saw young drug abusers come in with codependent parents who were trying to make life perfect to placate their manipulative and destructive children.

While I didn't drink or take drugs, my unpredictable behavior was often accompanied by inappropriate rages and was much like that of an alcoholic. Tom had been walking around on eggshells trying to keep the peace. He realized that we were both codependent.

Codependency, which is when someone completely relinquishes control of his or her emotions to someone else, isn't healthy for anyone. A person who feels his or her happiness, joy, sadness, hate or anger depends on what another person does or says or doesn't do or doesn't say. If you're solid and confident, then I can be, too, they mistakenly believe. But if you waver, then I waver even more. If you feel insecure, I feel terrified. If you aren't perfect, then my world is a mess.

Tom took very seriously Pastor Weaver's admonition that he was responsible to God for our relationship, and he first worked to correct his own failings. As he looked inside, Tom was surprised to discover that the new vehicles he purchased every two years or so, complete with hoods that could not be opened from the outside, were attempts to keep me safe from any further harm. Somewhere deep inside he believed that if I had been driving a better car that day, I wouldn't have been raped. He also recognized that fear—his fear—was at the heart of his extreme, controlling behavior, in which he closely monitored my comings and goings. Fear was also the reason Tom carefully scrutinized anyone he considered to be suspicious, even people just walking down the street. He had been trying to protect me from any unknown threat that loomed outside our door.

Most important, Tom came face-to-face with the sin of going after Hollabaugh with a knife while harboring murder in his heart. Tom thanked God for preventing him from carrying out his intentions that day, but it would be a long, long time before he shared any of that with me.

After his inward journey, Tom turned his attentions to helping me, and he began by standing his ground. If I threatened to run away after we'd had a fight, instead of pleading with me to stay, Tom would kiss me good-bye and tell me that he would miss me. He confronted head-on my every inappropriate behavior, which caused me to think hard about what I was saying and the reason I was saying it. And he did it all with love.

Tom combined this confrontation method with a technique he called "tripping-in," which just meant taking a trip inside to look at the deep feelings of fear or loss or pain that was at the heart of it all. At first it sounded like so much psychological jargon to me, but even as a skeptic, I had to admit that it worked, especially when Tom blended it with humor.

One day I was washing dishes while I was angry about something and kept slamming the cabinet doors and crashing one clean plate down upon another, all the while saying that nothing was wrong.

"You're being so harsh," Tom calmly said to me, walking out of the room and returning with our thesaurus. "In fact, let's look at how you are acting." Tom turned to the word "harsh" and began to read the synonyms. "You're so severe, so inharmonious, so sarcastic, so scathing, so stinging, so acrimonious," he said, mispronouncing the word.

"That's pronounced *a-kre-mo-ne-ous,*" I corrected him.

"Thanks. You're so brusque, so grating, so dry, so caustic," he said, mispronouncing again.

"That's pronounced *ko-stik,*" I corrected.

"Thanks. So oppressive, so trenchant . . ."

By this time we were both laughing and I realized he was right. I had been all those things, and the incident that caused the anger hadn't warranted such a response. I was beginning to learn how to look deep to find the real cause of my repressed, stuffed-down anger. Using humor to make me confront these issues was essential because we had learned that any show of anger from Tom, even when directed at someone else, would cause me to awaken screaming in the middle of the night from a nightmare that Tom was chasing me with a gun.

Tom's tripping-in technique was also effective in helping me remove the false belief systems that I had developed, which is very common for victims, especially if they suffered abuse when they were young. Victims often believe the abuse was their fault, that it wouldn't have happened if they had been prettier, nicer, successful, quieter, good, more outgoing, more helpful, or better in some way. When they grow up, this carries over in the way they interact with others. They want everyone to like them, they go to extremes to avoid arguments, they want to appear to the world as if they, and the people close to them, are perfect. This just sets them up to be victimized again.

For years I had believed that I was ugly. Every imperfection jumped out at me in the mirror. I looked at myself critically, thinking of how other people might view me, rather than seeing myself through God's eyes, perfect through Jesus Christ. I also wanted everything in my life to look perfect. I wanted Tom not to talk so much in public and have better table manners.

Tom finally said to me, "I'm not perfect. I'm never going to be perfect, and you need to come to terms with my imperfections if we are going to have a successful marriage."

Until then I hadn't realized I'd been expecting the impossible from my husband and from myself. I had given away too much power to others. If others thought we were a nice family, then we were. But if someone looked aghast when my gregarious husband talked too much, then that meant we weren't a nice family. I had been determining my value through the eyes of others, rather than through God.

Tom also helped me see that, like other victims, I was viewing parts of the Bible in a distorted way. Verses that advised Christians to turn the other cheek, lay your life down for your brother, love one another, carry one another's burdens, will keep a victim trapped if she or he doesn't step back and look at the context of each verse.

None of those verses meant I shouldn't be angry, but I had thought they had. I thought in order to be a good Christian, I couldn't feel angry at my rapist, especially when I had learned to stuff my feelings down deep inside. Instead, my anger became distorted and spilled out all over Tom, which is what counselors call displaced anger.

Tom showed me that anger is sometimes quite appropriate for Christians. The Bible makes a distinction between feeling angry, which is acceptable, and acting angry, cautioning, "in your anger, do not sin." Scripture shows us that anger is a reasonable response to having dignity stripped from you, but that it shouldn't lead to acts of revenge. The Bible also shows that our ability to forgive is dependent upon our honesty in dealing with the offense against us and on our own experience of God's forgiveness of our sin. I learned that I needed to express my feelings, especially the negative ones, in an appropriate way toward the proper person.

Of course, the biggest issue yet to be addressed was my inability to respond sexually to Tom, even when I desperately wanted to. Tom explained to me that sexual abuse victims usually either become promiscuous in an attempt to regain control, or they withdraw completely. I was in the latter group. In helping me overcome this major hurdle, Tom gave me total control in that area. He told me whatever we did together was totally up to me.

"You have power over me," Tom told me. "I relinquish all power to you. You can do whatever you want."

This freed me tremendously and I began to show my husband the love I had always felt for him. My defense mechanisms fell one by one by the wayside, and I began to grow stronger. I found myself actually standing my ground in arguments with Tom rather than running out the door or shutting myself up in the bathroom. I learned how to talk to Tom about issues, and I rejoiced in how strong our marriage had become.

And to sustain the changes that Tom and I had made, we bathed ourselves in the Word of God. However strong our resolve, human determination is weak at best. We can do it all by ourselves for a time, but soon we are "overtaken with a fault," as the Bible describes it. By aligning ourselves and our spirit with God, we are able to accomplish true change.

Hebrews 4:12 tells us: "For the word of God is living and active. Sharper than any double-edged sword, it penetrates even to dividing soul and spirit, joints and marrow; it judges the thoughts and attitudes of the heart."

When we allow the Word of God to shape our lives and our thoughts, it is as skillful as a surgeon's scalpel, carefully cutting away the disease and leaving intact the healthy parts. It exposes who we are, both good and bad, and what we think, either truth or lies. God's Word forces us to decide whether or not we will allow Him to shape our lives, our decisions, our motives, our intents, our actions and our behaviors. And when we see the truth in God's Word, the power of evil is broken.

We are given the Holy Spirit to help us in this journey. Romans 8:26 says: "In the same way, the Spirit helps us in our weakness. We do not know what we ought to pray for, but the Spirit himself intercedes for us with groans that words cannot express. And he who searches our hearts knows the mind of the Spirit, because the Spirit intercedes for the saints in accordance with God's will." Being a Christian doesn't mean we won't have trouble. But we are promised that God will go through our troubles with us.

Many years passed before I felt strong in my healing. Often I was impatient with God. I wanted him to either hurry up or just take me home to be with Him. I was tired of living in pain and discord. I would pray, God, You are omnipotent. You could make me whole, take away my pain and in an instant heal me. I have seen You do this upon occasion for others. Why won't You do this for me?

He soon answered me. I had been frying mozzarella sticks in deep, hot oil when the telephone rang. The caller was a girl in trouble, who was crying and needed help, and so I immediately began to pray with her. Soon I smelled smoke and realized the oil was about to catch fire. Still praying with her, I grabbed a pot holder and yanked the cast-iron skillet from the burner. The skillet burned through the cloth and into my hand. I jerked my hand back and the hot oil poured over my right wrist and melted my pink sweatshirt into my skin.

The pain was immediate and intense. I screamed and dropped the phone, writhing to the floor. My body immediately went into shock. I phoned Tom at his office but the line was busy. I had never in all my life felt such excruciating physical pain. The images around me—the stove, the pattern in the linoleum, the textured plastered walls—began to fade in and out. I was shaking. I finally got through on the phone, and within ten minutes, Tom, who has always been great in emergencies, was carrying me into the yard and packing my arm in snow. The relief was only momentary. When the burning continued, it was constant and intense, the pain burying deeper with each wave. I would have gladly died if that would have made the pain stop. This must be what hell will feel like, I thought.

My arm and hand blew up like a water balloon, only the balloon was my skin and the water my fluid. Any movement caused the fluid to slosh under my skin, and that nauseated me. When we arrived at the hospital emergency room, the pain was torturous. I spent that entire night in agony from the third-degree burns I had suffered.

The coming months brought grueling physical therapy. I cried every day for at least three months from pain, and because the doctors gave me little hope my hand would ever function normally again. I struggled with God every day. Lord, I prayed, I don't understand this. You're God. You could heal me instantly. You know how much I love pottery. You know I need my hands. I've dedicated these hands to serving You, in fact I've dedicated everything I do to You. What is this? And please note, I was ministering to someone when this happened. Haven't I gone through enough? And now I won't be able to use my hand? God, how could You allow this to happen to me?

For two hours every day, my physical therapist used a surgeon's scalpel to scrape away the dead skin cells. I received no painkiller and I thought I would die before it was over.

"Why do you have to keep doing this?" I asked him one day. My therapist was wonderful. I think he wanted to cry with me. "It is so painful, is it really necessary?"

"Oh, I could stop doing this anytime," he said.

Hearing that, I became angry and ready to fight, until he continued.

"I could stop so you wouldn't have the pain, but what I am doing allows the skin to heal properly. If we just leave you alone, you'll heal, but your skin will be gnarled and drawn and you may not have the full use of your arm. But if we make you go through the pain now, the skin will heal much better and be stronger than it was before. If you get hit in that spot, it won't hurt as much. The scar will be tough but elastic. I hate to do this to you every day, but I've seen hundreds of burn patients and I know what is best for you."

With that, I began to cry. I'm sure my therapist thought it was from the pain, but my tears were in response to hearing, from that example, the spiritual principle of God's healing. Deep inside me, a fountain let go. It was such a cleansing and accepting cry. God had used that experience to illustrate a very important principle to me: Sure, God can heal your pain instantly, Leisha. Or He could allow you to heal on your own, but the scars will be gnarly and drawn, tough and hardened. And in the future, when that same pain strikes, your agony will double. But if you heal properly with God and in His time, when you're hit in that spot again, you'll be elastic, pliable and even stronger.

I had an "Ah-ha" moment with God right there in the whirlpool and I received a peace I can't explain.

From that day, my healing proceeded much better than expected, and when I finished with therapy, to my doctor's great surprise, I gained full use of my right hand. I still have a nasty scar in the shape of a triangle, but it's strong and pliable. My doctor wanted me to have skin grafts, but that scar reminded me of the Trinity and of the lesson I learned. Whenever I feel pain, I need only look at that scar, think about Jesus' death on the cross and how the Trinity suffered that day and what His healing meant for us.

I have seen God heal others instantly. It does happen, but more often healing comes over time, through trials, through stubbing our toes, through a long-term process. A loving parent doesn't spoil his child. God cares more about building character in Him than healing quickly. He's concerned with the process. He wants us on our knees, seeking His face, asking His direction in our lives, becoming more like Him.

My healing took long years and much work. And during the process, we had our precious son, Alexander Clark, whose name means "strong, defender of men" and "learned, full of wisdom." From the moment he was born, Alex has ripped through life, healthy, strong and active. What a joy and what a blessing he has been to both Tom and me every day.

We also moved to Colorado, where Tom felt a call to go into ministry. The cross-country move with a very active toddler had been grueling. A couple of days after we arrived, Tom and I visited a local health club for a little rest, leaving Alex with Tom's brother Paul and our sister-in-law Kathy, with whom we were staying until we could find an apartment.

Tom and I sat in the hot tub, dazed by all that had happened so quickly and grateful for a quiet moment. I closed my eyes and nearly drifted off to sleep, but was roused by Tom's voice greeting a man who had just joined us. He was thin, had dark skin and dark hair and was in good physical condition. He spoke with an accent that sounded Spanish to me. Secretly I hoped my outgoing husband wouldn't get into a lengthy conversation. I was enjoying this rare quiet time.

"So you're an author," I heard Tom say. "And you're from New York? You sound Spanish. Hey, have you ever heard of the book *The Cross and the Switchblade?*"

"Well, yes. I've heard of it, I think," he replied. "I'm Puerto Rican." My interest was piqued and I sat up to join the conversation.

"This is my wife, Leisha," Tom said, gesturing toward me.

"Nice to meet you," he said in his broken, thick accent.

"Let me tell you about *The Cross and the Switchblade*," Tom began. The man listened with great interest and I noticed that he cracked several smiles as he listened.

"What did you say your name is?" Tom asked.

"I didn't, but it's Nicky," the man said.

At that I gave Tom a quick jab in the ribs. "Don't you know who this is?" I whispered. Looking up, I saw Nicky smile a roguish grin.

But Tom was on a single-minded mission to lead this man to Jesus Christ and he ignored my persistent elbow jabs and kicks beneath the water.

Inside, I began to laugh at the thought of Tom witnessing to Nicky Cruz, who just happened to be one of the main characters in *The Cross and the Switchblade*, which Tom was now describing in great detail. *The* Nicky Cruz, the one whose knife had been stopped by God's love. I had admired him greatly as a teenager and felt such a strong kinship with him still. This is too uncanny, I thought. I finally could take it no longer. I stopped Tom midsentence and grabbed his flailing arms that were emphasizing some point he was making.

"Don't you know who this is, Tom? This is Nicky Cruz!"

Nicky's face cracked a broad, slightly embarrassed grin. Tom's face went blank and then we all laughed uproariously.

"I was enjoying that," Nicky said. "Nobody's tried to lead me to Jesus in a very long time."

Nicky's sense of humor charmed us. He felt like an old, dear friend, not a brand-new one. I had been initially startled by his rough exterior, but soon learned that not too far beneath his gruffness was the sweet spirit of Jesus. Again I felt a kindred spirit with a man who I knew had walked through pain, rejection and harshness of life and was now on the other side with a strong and heartened faith. Again I found myself wishing for such power and strength in God. Nicky's gentleness had surprised me. I don't know what I had expected, perhaps a gang leader type, perhaps an older man with less zeal, but Nicky was none of those.

He had great energy, and gestured excitedly with his hands, especially when speaking of things of God. When God has done much in your life, it's only natural to be excited by Him.

We stood in the lobby of the health club for a very long time not wanting to leave our newfound friend. We explained how we had just moved to Colorado and that we were both looking for jobs and he told us he was looking for a good secretary. After he learned about my experience with Sam Butcher and Bill Biel of Precious Moments, his eyes widened, and the next day, I went to work for Nicky Cruz Outreach as his personal secretary.

Not long after I went to work there, I realized I had to tell him how his exchange with David Wilkerson on a New York street corner had saved my life.

"Did I ever tell you that you were my childhood hero?" I asked.

"Nah . . ." Nicky said, waving his hand at me.

"Yes, you were. Sometimes I can't believe I'm working for you. You had quite an impact on my life."

"Really, how?"

And I told him the story of my rape and how the words that David Wilkerson had used to stop Nicky's knife had also stopped my rapist and had probably saved my life.

"Wow! You should write that! You're a good writer."

"I might do that one day," I said.

Tom soon found work in a local hospital and began pursuing his interest in ministry during evenings and on weekends. We became very close to an older couple, Vernon and Martha Guttenfelder, who were associated with the Church of God. They became mentors to Tom, and under their guidance and with ten years of ministry under his belt, Tom became an ordained minister.

Tom and I began a Bible study in our apartment clubhouse and it grew so large that soon we were recognized as a church. We baptized many in our swimming pool. We were outgrowing the clubhouse, and a young man whose life had been radically changed after coming to Christ in that clubhouse introduced us to his father, who offered us free space in a building he owned.

I continued to share my story at doctors' meetings, garden clubs, civic groups and church groups. The more I shared my story, the more I became whole. But the stories I heard from other victims rocked my soul. I was overwhelmed by the pain. What I heard every time I spoke disturbed me the most. "I was raped and I've never told anyone," so many people told me, including a growing number of men.

The shame that is associated with sexual violation often keeps victims silent. Victims feel that the assault was their fault, or that they were in some way to blame, or that they should have fought back harder. I urged each person who whispered that secret in my ear to tell someone. I told them that they must share the pain for the healing to begin. No one can heal on his own.

Psalm 119:24: "Your testimonies also are my delight and my counselors."

I believe burying shame and believing those lies attacks our very soul. By keeping a secret deep within, there is no chance for healing.

God doesn't want us to feel ashamed. If I had to pick one Scripture as the key to my healing, it would be, "Yet if anyone suffers as a Christian, let him not be ashamed, but let him glorify God in this matter" (I Peter 4:16).

This Scripture was liberating. I rejoiced that I had no reason to be ashamed and I could glorify God with all that had happened to me by sharing with others about His mercy, His love and His healing grace.

"We are hard pressed on every side, yet not crushed; we are perplexed, but not in despair; persecuted, but not forsaken; struck down, but not destroyed—always carrying about in the body the dying of the Lord Jesus, that the life of Jesus also may be manifested in our body" (2 Corinthians 4:8–10).

We all have trouble in common. Anyone living and breathing will have some kind of trouble in life. And if it's not here yet, it's on its way. And I intimately knew trouble. I had walked hand in hand with it my whole life, but I also knew a comforter. As I spoke, I met many people who hadn't, and desire began to grow to introduce others to the God of all comfort. As Paul said in 2 Corinthians 1:2–4, "Grace to you and peace from God our Father and the Lord Jesus Christ. Blessed be the God and Father of our Lord Jesus Christ, the Father of mercies and God of all comfort, who comforts us in all our tribulation, that we may be able to comfort those who are in any trouble, with the comfort with which we ourselves are comforted by God."

God granted me the desires of my heart shortly afterward. A representative from Pat Robertson's 700 Club television show called and invited me to share my story on national television. I was thrilled.

I immediately called my dear prayer partners and asked that they pray for me. Although we lived in different parts of the country, we were a tight collection of friends. We had met as we had traveled for business or church meetings and had become extraordinarily close. We counted heavily on each other for prayer. We later called ourselves the Peas and Carrots society because one of our members, Sandy, liked to eat her vegetables all mixed up. One day she gushed, "Oh, I love it when we're all together. It's like having all my peas and carrots at the same time."

Covered by their prayers, I felt confident when an entire production crew flew to Colorado and spent several days interviewing me and taping my story.

As I contemplated this great blessing, I mentally took a step back and realized that I was pretty comfortable with my life. I had a precious son whom both Tom and I greatly loved. My marriage had healed, and the healing of my spirit was continuing every day. My only problem was my continuing illnesses.

Uncontrollable bleeding had forced me to quit my job with Nicky Cruz, and sometimes my headaches were so severe Tom had to pack my head in ice. Not long afterward, I had to have a hysterectomy. Health problems had always plagued me. But despite those things, God, I'm finally happy, I prayed silently. Grace has many, many shades and I think I've seen them all.

It was only a day or two later that Kelly, my brother Kenny's wife, telephoned us from their Michigan home.

"A detective stopped by our house today looking for you," she said. "He wanted your phone number but I didn't want to give it to him until I talked with you first."

"What did he want?"

"I'm not sure. It was something about the rape case. Maybe you should call him, I took his number. His name is Mike Terry and he came up from South Carolina."

Lord, I silently prayed before I dialed his number, what now?

He answered the phone on the first ring. "Hello, Mike Terry," he said in a deep southern accent.

"Mr. Terry, this is Leisha Joseph."

"Well, hello," he said cheerfully. "I've been looking for you."

"I know. My sister-in-law called me. I understand you were at their house."

"Yes, I was. I hate to bring this back up in your life, but I understand you were influential in helping put Donald Hollabaugh behind bars the first time."

"The first time? What do you mean? He's in prison."

"Well, he *was* in prison. He's gotten out and—"

"What do you mean he's gotten out? Why wasn't I told?"

"Well, let me just tell ya. It's pretty messed up, but he started seeing this female counselor while in prison. She helped him get an early parole for good behavior. She helped draft him a résumé and he got a good job when he got out. He's been traveling for his job and we think he's been committing the same crime with the same M.O."

"M.O.?"

"Oh, modus operandi, method of operation. In other words, we think he's doing the very same thing he did up in Ohio. He tried to rape a girl here in South Carolina, but I'll tell ya, we don't mess around down here in the South. Somebody saw him jump this girl and he pulled him out of the car, beat him to a bloody pulp and literally sat on him until the police got there."

"Well, hallelujah for the South!"

"Yeah, down here we don't mess around with guys like him. Only thing is, you see, he didn't actually rape her, so the only case we have against him is kidnapping and aggravated assault with a deadly weapon."

"Did he use a gun again?"

"No, he put a screwdriver to her throat."

"Was she hurt at all?"

"No."

"Thank God."

"The thing is, I'm a detective for the North Augusta Police Department helping to investigate this case. I went up to Toledo and I dug through his records. I went into the basement of the courthouse and poked around through the microfiche and I came across your name. It seems you got something that scares him. Whatever it is, we need it. We want to get this guy and we need your help."

"What do you mean? What do I have to do with this case?"

"He committed the same M.O. He pulled her distributor wires on her car and waited for her to come out of the store. We think we have some fingerprints on the hood of the car, but we need your corroborating testimony. If we get a kidnapping charge to stick, it carries a mandatory life sentence in South Carolina."

"What do you mean, 'if'?"

"Well, kidnapping is hard to prove, that's why we need your help. We'll take care of you while you're here."

"I'll have to think about this. You know I've wrestled with this for eleven years. I've prayed for him nearly every day, but he's caused me a lot of grief. I've really just gotten back on my feet. I just taped the *700 Club* and it's scheduled to air in a month, this very story. I'll have to discuss this with my husband, think about it and call you back."

"Okay, I understand. I hope to hear from you real soon."

As I hung up the phone, I felt like I was sinking in quicksand. How can this be, Lord? You've taken me from church basements because the church hierarchy was too embarrassed by the topic to put me in the sanctuary, to sharing my story on national TV on the *700 Club*. In eleven years You've taught me so much. Do I really have to face him again? He's robbed me of so much. Darn it! This just isn't fair! Will I ever be rid of him?

I took a long walk in the mountains. I walked and walked for miles. It was nearly dark and I still didn't want to go home. I just wanted to get lost in thick pine trees, crawl under some bush and close my eyes. If it weren't for my Alex and Tom, Lord, I'd just walk off one of these mountaintops.

The response was clear and strong: The Lord is my light and my salvation; Whom shall I fear?

Yes, Lord, I know that full well.

What shall you fear when I'm with you?

Are You with me, Lord? Are You?

Yes.

Okay. We can do this together, but I need You more than ever. I took a long breath, drawing deep into my lungs the crisp fresh air that was heavily scented with pine. The evergreens and the aspens were towering silhouettes against the night sky as I slowly began to walk down the mountain path. The leaves and twigs crunching beneath my feet were the only sounds I heard as I began to pray: Rejuvenate him, Lord. Open his seared conscience. Let him know his depravity. Let him fall on his face before You and know that You are God.

Chapter 10

THE
LITTLE
FOXES

*"Catch for us the foxes,
the little foxes
that ruin the vineyards,
our vineyards that are in bloom."*

SONG OF SONGS
2:15 (NIV)

For Tom there was no question. Of course I had to testify. But he insisted on going with me.

"Call that detective back and tell him you'll come, but only if I come, too," Tom said. "I'm not going to let you go through this alone."

With God's comfort and my husband's support, my heart was filled with peace the next day as I picked up the telephone and dialed the South Carolina telephone number.

"This is Mike Terry."

"Hi, Mike. It's Leisha."

"Been waiting to hear from you."

"Look, you can't guarantee me that he won't walk, right?"

"Well . . ."

"I know you can't guarantee me that, so here's the deal. I'll come, but only under my conditions."

"And they are?"

"You arrange the trip for me and my husband, take care of all our expenses and assure me that I can give Hollabaugh a gift."

"A gift! What kinda gift?"

"I'd rather not say at this point, but that's the deal."

"Okay, well, let me do some checking around here on how that would work and get back to you."

Before Mike called back, I went to the local Christian bookstore. "I want the best leather Bible you have. It's a very special gift."

"For someone close to you?"

"Well, I guess you could say that."

From somewhere, I believe from heaven, the idea had come to buy Hollabaugh a Bible. My very own, worn-down, dog-eared, soft-as-a-glove Bible was so many things to me: it was my friend, my weapon, the truth, it provided clarification and meaning to life. I believed if I put the Word of God into Hollabaugh's hands, then I had done my part. I had done everything I could possibly do to protect my family. And, of course, it was my prayer that he might open it one day and ask God for rejuvenation.

"This is the best one we have. It's a top-grade, leather study Bible and inside, Jesus' words are highlighted in red."

"Great, that's the one I want. Now, I want this name, Donald Hollabaugh, engraved in gold letters on the front cover. Can you do that?"

"Sure."

"Then I need you to help me pray over this Bible."

"I'd be happy to."

All the clerks gathered around the counter and laid their hands on the Bible. By then my story was fairly well known in our small community, and after I told them this latest twist, many of them became teary-eyed as we prayed. I took the Bible with me to church that night and the entire congregation laid hands on the Bible and prayed. I was confident this was among the most anointed Bibles ever.

Later that day Mike called me back. The team had agreed with my conditions and had arranged for me to give the gift through Hollabaugh's attorney after the trial.

Within days, Alex went to stay with Jim and Melanie Tangelder, our friends who lived deep in the Colorado mountains, in gold mining country. Our dog, Stubby, went to the kennel and off we went to the airport. It was a quiet flight, neither of us talked much. I think we both felt a little weary already, knowing what lay ahead, but not knowing what the outcome would be.

We picked up a rental car at the airport and then drove to a one-pump gas station outside the small town of Aiken, South Carolina, where we would meet Mike. We got there on time, but Mike was nowhere to be seen. As we sat there waiting, quiet in our thoughts, mine began to run amok. What if this was a setup? I hadn't considered that. What if Hollabaugh had escaped and this was just a ploy to bring us here? What if Mike Terry is his brother or cousin or some relative. I hadn't really checked him out.

My thoughts were interrupted as a speeding Mustang screeched into the gas station.

"That's him," Tom said.

"How can you tell?"

"The car. It's a 5.0-liter, high-performance engine. Only a cop would drive a car like that."

"Are you sure? I'm so glad you're street-smart. That Detroit upbringing comes in handy sometimes."

Tom jumped out of the car and quickly walked to the Mustang. Mike stuck out his big hand and they greeted one another. His warmth and friendliness made me feel like I was being welcomed by some distant cousin who couldn't wait to shower us with southern hospitality.

"Y'all follow me and I'll show you 'round town so you can get your bearings before we go to the hotel."

We followed him on a brief tour of the town. It was lovely. The lush lawns and the spreading trees all seemed a richer shade of green than I was accustomed to seeing. Many of the homes on the canopied streets were old and cozy with large, wraparound porches and hanging Boston ferns. So many of them looked like they should be listed in the national historic building registry. The air smelled so sweet, could it be honeysuckle or maybe lilacs?

Ashley, the victim witness coordinator, met us at the hotel. Mike had told me that I would be enrolled in the witness protection program and assigned a caseworker who would inform me of any changes in Hollabaugh's status if he were convicted. This time, if he got out again, for any reason, I would be notified.

"Please just let us know if you need anything," Ashley said. Both she and Mike were very accommodating. Their gentle, down-home style and easy way of speaking made me feel like I was among friends.

The first day of the trial was scheduled to begin early in the morning, so we decided to go right to our room. Tom fell asleep immediately, but I was too unsettled. My mind kept dredging up the face that I would have to see the next morning; the face that I would never forget; the one that had, for years, haunted my dreams. What will it feel like to sit that close to him again? I wondered. I didn't get much sleep that night.

Lord, can I do this? You promised You'd never give me more than I could handle. You promised to be with me. My fretfulness nudged my husband from his sleep.

"Honey? Are you okay?" Tom asked me.

"No."

"Come here," he said, hugging me close in his big, strong arms. "I am with you. God is with you. And you are doing exactly what He wants you to be doing right now. You are being obedient and you are serving God. Dear Lord, I pray that You pour an extra measure of comfort on Leisha . . ."

I fell asleep in Tom's arms listening to him pray for me.

We got up early and Tom had a good breakfast, but I couldn't eat a thing. As we walked into the large, majestic courthouse, I clung to Tom with one hand while the other gripped the leather Bible that I was bringing as a gift to my rapist.

We walked down the wide hallway, and the hollow echo of my shoes on the marble floor drummed in my ears. Could I do this? Mike was waiting by the courtroom and escorted us to a room where we met the assistant district attorney, Lawrence Brown. He was much younger than I'd expected. He looked eighteen, though he spoke like a much older and wiser man.

"Look at this, Leisha," Mike said, showing me Hollabaugh's doctored résumé that he'd used to get a job. "Look here, he put himself inside the correctional institutions during the time he was in prison, but he says he was working there as an 'administrative assistant.' "

I took the two-page résumé and shook my head at the boldness. For 1983 through 1987, which would have been when he was in prison for my rape, Hollabaugh said he was an administrative assistant at the Lebanon Correctional Institution. Hollabaugh's résumé said he "assisted in the rewriting of multi-faceted security procedures which are still in effect. Drafted and acted as overseer of $750,000 custody budget, which included the computerization of all custody department transactions." He also listed that he "heard confidential union grievance complaints and made recommendations for action within the framework of ongoing union negotiations and present union contract" and that he "acted as liaison between Institutional personnel and Wilmington College campus staff." And lastly, Hollabaugh said his references were available upon request. I sure would have liked to see those.

"Totally bogus," Mike said. "His girlfriend helped him write it. She was some counselor he was seeing at the prison as part of his treatment. Then when companies called the prison to check on him, she verified his story."

"Amazing" was all my usually verbose husband could say.

Mike also introduced Tom and me to Suzanne, Hollabaugh's latest victim, and to her family, who was there with her. We also met Barbara, the district attorney of the Second Judicial Circuit, who was Lawrence's boss, Tom the investigating officer and several others who had worked diligently on the case.

I looked at Suzanne and remembered what it felt like to be a victim. I knew every thought she was having. I felt every tear she was holding back. I wanted to hug her and tell her how the Lord helped me through my experience. I wanted to hold her until the pain subsided. Deep compassion surged inside me, but I knew this wasn't the time for comfort. The best thing I could do for her was help put Donald Hollabaugh away once more. The familiar righteous indignation flooded back and I was on the warpath again. I searched for the nervousness that had fluttered without restraint in my stomach moments earlier and realized that it had retreated in deference to a stronger emotion. Strength surged through me and I began to see my higher purpose for being there.

I remembered a conversation I had with Jim Wilson, my dear friend and mentor in business.

"Leisha," he once said to me, "God's not transactional. He's transformational. You may think you're going to Chicago next week to nail a business transaction. But God has some greater, transforming business in mind. You have a powerful life message and whether you land this contract or not, your presence allows for change. You may only have this one moment in time to affect a person's life."

I realized that this was the kind of opportunity Jim had been talking about. This was a moment in time I could bring transforming power into some lives. Regardless of the outcome of the trial, that's what I intended to do.

"Mike," I said impatiently, "when can I give him my gift?"

"Not until the trial is over. He may cause a scene or attack you or spit on you or something. It's best if we wait until everything is over. We've made arrangements with his lawyer to give it to him after the trial."

Tom and I sat in the front row with Suzanne and her family. We waited for the proceedings to begin as lawyers huddled together and rustled papers and others gathered for hushed conversations around the room.

Finally, the Honorable Judge Hubert Long addressed the jury. From the first moment he opened his mouth, it was obvious that Judge Long ran a laid-back, comfortable courtroom. He was the charming combination of a keen, knowledgeable arbitrator and a country boy with down-home wit and common sense. Motions overruled or sustained were often accompanied by amusing commentary.

Judge Long explained the structure of court days, how many breaks the jury would have, and that they should raise their hands when they had to go to the rest room.

"We're back in school," he said. "So be it."

He reminded the lawyers to stand back so the jury could hear the testimony, and he cautioned the jury not to discuss the case, not to watch television or read the newspapers during the trial, which was expected to last several days.

"And let me say this: Number one, before I forget it, since only four people out of the whole panel have ever been on a jury, at the end of the case when your verdict is arrived at—you're a long ways from that. That's the last thing. When you arrive at the verdict, you knock on the door because I had the experience one time where nobody on the jury had served and the foreman came out and said, 'How long we got to stay in here after we arrived at the verdict?' And I said, 'What's that?' And he said, 'We agreed on the verdict three hours ago, how long we got to stay in here?' Nobody knew to knock on the door so they sat in there three hours. I just took it for granted, but you don't take things for granted. Obviously nobody on that jury had ever been in the courtroom, you see. So I say, knock on the door."

The judge went on to explain that any rulings he made had nothing to do with taking sides, that he was there to make sure the law was followed. And at the end of the trial, he would explain the law to the jury and then they would be the final judges as to what was true.

Suzanne was the first one called to the witness stand. She testified that she had been at work and had gone to a local tanning salon during her lunch break. She had just come out of the salon and tried to start her car. When it failed to start, she noticed that the hood was ajar.

"I knew I had not driven over there with my hood open. I got out and looked underneath and didn't notice anything wrong, so I closed it completely and got back in the car and tried to start it again and it wouldn't start. And that's when Mr. Hollabaugh came up and offered help."

"When did you first see him?" Mr. Brown asked.

"I did not see him walk up to the car. He was just there. I guess he came from behind me because I didn't see him approach the car. I just looked at my side and he was there. And he said, 'Ma'am, are you having car trouble?' And I said, 'Yes.' And he said, 'Well, could I help you?' And I started out of the car and he kneeled down and was halfway in my car and messed with some wires that were hanging down underneath my steering wheel."

Mr. Brown asked if she could identify him and Suzanne pointed to Hollabaugh.

She testified that after he worked with the wires, he told her to get in the car and try to start it again. When she did, he pushed her down on the seat, got in with her and locked the door. She felt the screwdriver pushing deep into her neck and he told her not to scream or he would kill her.

"I thought he was going to drive me away, rape me, kill me and leave me," she testified.

Suzanne said she pleaded with Hollabaugh to take her money, jewelry and her car, but to please not kill her.

"And that made him very angry," she testified. "He didn't like to hear me speak. Whenever I spoke, he applied pressure to my chest. And he said, 'Just get in the backseat.'"

"What did you do when he told you to get in the backseat?"

Suzanne testified that she had remembered seeing a woman using the public telephone between the tanning booth and her car, and told Hollabaugh she would get into the backseat just so she could raise up and try to get the woman's attention. When she did, the woman looked over and saw her. His attention diverted, Suzanne began to scream and kick on the car window.

"What did he do then?" Mr. Brown asked.

"He called me a bitch and got out of the car. He let me go. And I think we got out of the car at the same time and I ran and grabbed the woman who was on the telephone and ran into the tanning salon."

I had been watching the jury. They had been leaning forward, listening to Suzanne with great interest. And now it was time for Hollabaugh's attorney, Elmer Hatcher, to try to lay a foundation for some doubt in their minds. Mr. Hatcher asked Suzanne how long she and Hollabaugh had been in the car together that day.

"About seven minutes," Suzanne answered.

"So he held a screwdriver to your throat, you were yelling and kicking and screaming, and all of this was going on for seven minutes with a full parking lot in the middle of the afternoon with somebody standing twenty-five feet away on the telephone?" Mr. Hatcher asked.

"Yes."

"Seven minutes?"

"Yes."

Mr. Hatcher then showed Suzanne a copy of the statement she had made to police in which she said a knife had been placed at her throat. Suzanne explained that she had felt a sharp point and assumed Hollabaugh had a knife, but later read in the newspaper that the weapon had been a screwdriver.

With a great deal of drama, Hatcher pointed out that Suzanne didn't need any medical treatment after the attack and that she had not even broken a fingernail.

"So, you're saying for seven minutes a man much larger than you assaulted you with the intent to kill you and did not leave a mark on your body?"

"Yes."

"Do you have any idea, by the way, how he planned on kidnapping you in a vehicle that wouldn't start?"

"At the time, I didn't know the car would not start. I figured he fixed it and we were going to drive away."

The jury was still listening intently when Mr. Hatcher finished. The next witness was Angela, a store cashier who testified that she had been using the public telephone during a break when she saw Suzanne kick the car window. Angela said she ran toward the store, screaming, "Somebody come help her!" Then she saw a man who was already running toward Suzanne's car.

Jana, who works at the tanning salon, was next called to the witness stand. She testified she and Suzanne had left the salon at about the same time because Jana's husband, Bobby, had arrived to talk to her. The couple heard Suzanne's car engine grinding, then they heard her car hood slam. Bobby started to go offer help when they saw Hollabaugh approach her and they assumed someone else was giving her a hand. As they talked, they noticed that Hollabaugh seemed to be working with some wires beneath the dashboard, then they saw him shove Suzanne into the car. Seconds later, they heard Suzanne screaming. Jana testified that she ran into the salon to call the police and Bobby ran to help Suzanne.

During his questioning, Mr. Hatcher emphasized the point that Jana had neglected to tell the police that she had seen Hollabaugh fiddling with the wires beneath the dashboard. He suggested that she didn't want to lose business and was merely supporting the testimony of a good customer.

"I would support it if it were the truth," Jana replied.

Bobby was called to the witness stand. He testified that he had been working on his car on his day off and realized he needed to buy some parts to make repairs. He loaded his three children into the car and drove to the tanning salon to get money from Jana. The children waited in the car as he and Jana talked. Bobby testified that they saw Suzanne try to start her car, and that Jana told him not to leave because Suzanne might need help. He said he saw Hollabaugh approach and appear to help Suzanne. But when Hollabaugh shoved Suzanne into the car and got in next to her, Bobby said he knew something was wrong. After he heard her scream and saw her kicking the car window, Bobby ran to help. By that time both Hollabaugh and Suzanne were getting out of the car. Bobby testified that Hollabaugh looked like he was "fixing to run. He was in a stride like he had somewhere else to be real quick."

"I grabbed hold of him and we went to the ground," Bobby testified.

"Why did you hold him down?" Mr. Brown asked.

"All I knew was something was wrong. The girl at the phone was screaming and hollering and something was wrong. It just didn't look right."

"Did Donald Hollabaugh do anything when you grabbed him?"

"Tried to get up."

"What did you do?"

"Held him on the ground."

"How big are you?" Mr. Brown asked.

"Six two; weigh about a hundred sixty pounds."

"He's a lot bigger than you are?"

"I would say so."

"How did you hold him down?"

"I had him by his neck, or collar of his jacket, and shoved him toward the ground."

"And did he just stay there peacefully?" Mr. Brown asked.

"No, sir."

"What did he do?"

"He tried to press himself up as if he was trying to do push-ups with me on his back."

"And what did you do?"

"I stepped on his hands."

"Why did you do that?"

"Well, I realized I had grabbed something bigger than I was."

"After you stepped on his hands, did he give you any trouble?"

"No, sir."

"And how long did you have to hold him until the police arrived?"

"About three to four minutes."

"The whole time you were holding him down, was he quiet?"

"He kept asking me to let him up, saying he had not done anything. Well, I had seen different, so I felt I should hold him until proper authorities had gotten there."

"What kind of shape were you in when all of this was going on?" Mr. Brown asked.

"What do you mean by that?" Bobby asked.

"I mean emotionally."

"I was a little upset. Strung-out. I was wired up over it."

"And after you turned him over to the police, what did you do?"

"I went and found somewhere to be alone."

"Okay, were you ever around the car when the police were out there looking around?" Mr. Brown asked.

"Yes."

"Did you find anything when you were out there?"

"A screwdriver that was underneath a gray or brown pickup that was parked right next to her."

"And where did you find the screwdriver?"

"Found it underneath the center of the truck around the rear axle."

"What did you do when you found the screwdriver?"

"Nothing. I just notified the officers that were there."

"Could you identify that screwdriver again if you saw it?" Mr. Brown asked.

"I believe so."

"Can you identify that?" Mr. Brown asked, pointing to the screwdriver on the table.

"That was the screwdriver that was under the back of the gray truck," Bobby said.

"Your Honor, we would ask that be marked as State's Exhibit Number Fourteen."

"Any objection?" asked Judge Long.

"I'd like the opportunity to cross-examine him about the screwdriver," Mr. Hatcher said.

"Well, any objection as far as introducing it?" Judge Long asked. "You've got a right to cross-examination."

"Yes, sir. I don't believe the identification has been proper," Mr. Hatcher said. "I mean, how can you tell one screwdriver from another? Unless they go through the chain of evidence or something, I don't see how he can say that's the particular screwdriver."

"He said it was the particular screwdriver. Isn't that what he said?" asked Judge Long.

"Yes, sir," Mr. Hatcher said.

"Well, that's his testimony," said Judge Long. "Admit it."

The screwdriver was marked and entered into evidence over Mr. Hatcher's objection.

When it was his turn for questions, Mr. Hatcher spent several minutes pointing out that during his testimony Bobby had once referred to Hollabaugh as "the subject," in an attempt, I believe, to suggest he was repeating what police had told him to say. Hatcher then questioned Bobby about how he had detained Hollabaugh. Mr. Hatcher lay on the courtroom floor and asked Bobby to stand on his hands the way he had stood on Hollabaugh's.

Even Judge Long appeared surprised. "If you want him to really step on your fingers . . ." he interrupted.

"I want him to put his feet in the position they were in," Mr. Hatcher confirmed.

"All right. I'll stay out of it," Judge Long replied.

In his demonstration, Mr. Hatcher showed that Bobby couldn't have stood as he had described for three or four minutes, as he had testified.

"He wasn't really trying to get away from you, was he?" Mr. Hatcher asked.

"I felt he was."

"He's a lot bigger than you, isn't he?"

"Yes, sir."

"All right. You said you were strung-out and wired. Right?"

"Right."

"On what?"

"Adrenaline."

"Adrenaline? Isn't strung-out and wired terms people normally use about drugs?"

"Objection, Your Honor!" Mr. Brown said. "That's totally improper on Mr. Hatcher's part."

Mr. Hatcher turned his attention to Bobby's memory. He handed him a copy of the statement he had given to police, and pointed out that Bobby hadn't told police that he had seen Suzanne slam the hood of her car.

"This is just a big game of cops and robbers to you, isn't it?"

"No, sir."

"Then why have you changed at least two things you've testified to on the stand? You recognize this is the most important thing in a man's life, don't you?"

"Yes, sir."

"I don't have any further questions."

By then the pattern and the intent of Mr. Hatcher's line of questioning had become clear to Tom and me: beat up the good guys. Here, clearly, was a hero. Bobby had bolted across a parking lot, tackled a man who outweighed him by seventy pounds, put his own life at risk in order to stop an attack on a small, defenseless woman. And this champion's character, his motives, his memory, were under assault. Tiny, insignificant details were exaggerated, minor inconsistencies were held up as lies and omissions, and presented as evidence of character flaws.

Clearly, Bobby was a very brave man. He was a hero. I wished with all my heart that someone like him had been in the Bargain City parking lot on July 3, 1979, for me. With the nips and nibbles of little foxes, we could see that Mr. Hatcher was eating away at the cold facts. It was all so unfair and there seemed to be no way to stop it. The faces of the jurors were changing, too. We could see questions and doubt beginning to form in their eyes. Why in our system does it seem like the criminals have all the rights and the victims have none?

O Lord, I prayed, it's not like that with You. Let Your Word shine down and reveal the deceptive hearts of the little foxes. Expose the truth.

Every day, I carried the Bible to court with me, tucked beneath my arm, eager for the chance to present it to Hollabaugh. He had glanced at Tom and me a couple of times. I was thankful that Tom by then was a seasoned Christian and was able to withstand the looks without jumping to defend me.

The next day a string of police officers and experts testified. Officer Wayne Duke said he found a roll of white surgical tape, a pair of latex gloves and a pair of ladies' stockings stuffed in Hollabaugh's pockets when he was searched at the police station.

None of those items were needed for Hollabaugh's job as a field trainee for O.H. Materials, a hazardous-waste cleanup company, his supervisor testified. Hollabaugh had been on the job for about two weeks and had just been sent to Beaufort, South Carolina, for on-the-job training in the field accounting division. The day he was arrested, he was supposed to have been picking up supplies in Aiken, the supervisor testified.

Officer Robbie Bell testified that he and Sergeant Tom Rogers discovered that a coil wire had been disconnected from the distributor of Suzanne's vehicle, and that they had found Hollabaugh's palm print on the hood, near the latch mechanism that was beneath the grille.

Suzanne, Jana, Angela and Bobby had all testified previously that Hollabaugh had not gone near the hood of the car when he approached Suzanne. The implication, of course, was that Hollabaugh had opened the car hood and yanked the coil wire while Suzanne was in the tanning salon and lay in wait for her to return. The story had a familiar and eerie ring to me. I looked at the jury. They appeared to be sincere, dedicated citizens who were, no doubt, there because they wanted to perform a service to their community. But I could see that they didn't understand what nearly had happened to Suzanne. I was the only one in that courtroom who had experienced what Hollabaugh would have done to Suzanne if she had gone into the backseat of the car with him.

By the third day of trial, fourteen witnesses had been called, and the testimony droned on. Mr. Hatcher often spent long minutes hammering some poor witness on an obscure point, the meaning of which was often lost to most of us. A great deal of time was dedicated to explaining how fingerprints are taken, how they are photographed and how the police department can assure that confiscated evidence hasn't been tampered with. It was all important, but hours upon hours of testimony dulled the senses.

"The jury has seen a couple of exhibits of a palm print and I was just wondering if you would tell us, just what is a fingerprint?" Mr. Brown asked Larry Gainey, an undisputed fingerprint expert who had studied with the FBI.

"Well, on the palm surface of your hand from the tips of your fingers to your wrist there are raised portions of skin. This skin is known as friction ridge skin. And when this friction ridge skin, which constantly exudes perspiration which is mostly water, oils and some salts, comes in contact with a surface, it may leave a fingerprint or it may leave a print. It could be a palm print. That depends on the condition of the surface touch. For instance . . ."

As Gainey talked on, I looked at the jury. "Look," I whispered, nudging Tom. "Some of those jurors are falling asleep."

Sure enough, the soft light in the courtroom combined with the gentle murmur of continuous testimony was lulling a few of them to sleep. They were nodding in their chairs.

"He's going to walk," I whispered. "They don't get it. They don't know what that girl had in store for her."

Tom patted my hand. "God's in control, Leisha. And they haven't heard from you yet."

Gainey talked for about ten more minutes before concluding, "I charted twenty-four characteristics on this particular display. However, there are over fifty corresponding characteristics between the latent print and the inked print."

"So both of those prints belong to Donald Hollabaugh?"

"Yes, sir. They do."

After a brief cross-examination, in which Mr. Hatcher pointed out that many prints taken off the car were not Donald Hollabaugh's, Judge Long called a recess.

"We're going to take a break and there are some matters of law I need to take up," he told the jury. "I have no idea how long it will take, but I've been made aware, so we'll be back as soon as we can. Again, Mr. Foreman, make certain nobody talks about the case."

The jury was led out of the room and I discovered that the "matters of law" concerned me.

"Your Honor, we intend on calling Leisha Joseph as a witness," Mr. Brown began.

"Calling who?" Judge Long interrupted.

"Leisha Joseph, who will give testimony as to the motive, intent, prior course of conduct."

"Well, now, I need to know exactly what she is going to say and what area she's going to cover, because I must make a ruling on that," Judge Long said. "Then, if she says something beyond the area of scope, I'll declare a mistrial if it's prejudicial. You understand?"

That initiated a long discussion between the judge and the two attorneys during which rules, laws and old and new cases were cited.

Mr. Hatcher was adamant in his opposition to my testifying. His main objection was that the prosecution had to prove that the probative value, or what would be learned by my testimony, would outweigh the prejudicial effect I would have on the jury.

"There is no way in the world that we could introduce evidence here of something that happened back in Ohio eleven years ago without the jury coming to the conclusion that if he did it once, he's going to do it again," Mr. Hatcher said.

That, of course, is exactly what I was hoping for, deep in my heart.

Mr. Brown cited current case law that said testimony could be given if the previous crime and the charged offense were similar in the way they were carried out. "Your Honor, in this case the circumstances are as nearly identical as I could ever imagine them being, down to and including the fact that while Mrs. Joseph was being assaulted by the defendant, there were passers-by who went by her car."

"All right, just let me say this. Gentlemen, I'll rule," Judge Long said. "Now, Elmer . . . I should say Mr. Hatcher, but I know both of y'all's father and families and all, pardon my unjudicial thing. I'm going to order that it not come out about the rape, that you lead up to the point that the assault was, that he pushed her down and stop at that. Now, you understand what I'm saying?"

"Yes, sir," Mr. Hatcher said. "First of all, I except to her being allowed to testify at all."

"No question about it," Judge Long replied.

"And I have a continuous objection to her entire testimony."

"That's right," Judge Long said. "Make certain that the young lady understands because we do not want her to cross that barrier. Anyhow, we all understand, so shut up. Y'all ready to proceed?"

"Your Honor, may I have just a couple of minutes to speak to her before the jury comes in to clarify that?" asked Mr. Brown.

"All right," said Judge Long.

Lawrence pulled me aside and cautioned me not to mention the rape. "We'll have a mistrial, for sure," he said. "And I don't want that, Leisha."

"I understand."

"Are you ready to testify?"

"I will be in a minute," I said. "There's something I have to do first."

Chapter 11

LET
JUSTICE
ROLL
DOWN

*"But let justice roll on like a river,
righteousness like a never-failing stream!"*

— AMOS 5:24 (NIV)

Court was still in recess as I walked down the long, marble hallway to the ladies' room. I pressed my hot forehead against the cool wall and closed my eyes.

God, I prayed, You saw those jurors. They were asleep! Lord, they don't understand what he intended to do to that poor girl. You know, Lord. You know what's in his heart. God, I ask You to give me the words to sway that jury. You've done this twice and I ask You to do it again. If I can't tell them with my words what would have happened to Suzanne, then use my body language. Let them see it in my eyes, let them hear it in the intensity of my voice or the gestures of my hands. Lord, help me to make them understand the full implications of his crime, what he would have done to her, what he will do again to someone else if they set him free. Dear Lord, let justice roll down.

My heart was thumping in my chest as I walked back into the courtroom to wait my turn to speak.

"Call your next witness," Judge Long said.

"We call Leisha Joseph, Your Honor," Mr. Brown said.

I was witness number 15, and the last to testify. I walked to the witness stand, raised my hand and swore to tell the truth.

And so, once more, I told my story, and this time, before a very important audience. Just as before in that Ohio courtroom, the words poured forth with all the confidence, strength and power of the truth.

Mr. Brown asked me to identify my attacker, and before I did, I glanced at the jury. Each one was listening intently, many leaning forward. Some of their eyes were opened wide.

I pointed to Hollabaugh. "He's wearing a gray suit with a grayish brown tie." From his place at the defense table, Hollabaugh glared at me. He was more subtle than he had been in the Ohio courtroom, but I could still feel the intensity of his stare. I looked at him full in the face. I could feel the conviction shining in my eyes. He looked away.

"And what happened when he asked if he could help you?" Mr. Brown asked.

"He reached down and he said, 'Well, let me try to start it.' And at the same time I felt something hard go into my ribs."

"Did you see what it was?"

"It was a gun."

I thought I heard someone on the jury gasp.

"Did he get in the car?" Mr. Brown asked.

"Yes, he did. He closed the door behind him."

"And what did you do?"

"I started praying out loud. At that point he had moved the gun up to my throat. I prayed even louder. The more I spoke, the angrier he became. He told me to shut up. I told him I was a Christian and that made him angrier."

"Made him angrier? Did he say anything to you about that?"

"He shoved the gun up into my throat and said, 'Shut up or I'm going to blow you into a million pieces.' "

"And what did you do?"

"Well, I had heard the testimony of David Wilkerson when Nicky Cruz put a knife to his throat and said he was going to cut him in a million pieces. And David Wilkerson said, 'Just go ahead and every piece will still love you.' And Nicky stopped what he was doing, and I remembered that from when I was a teenager."

"And is that what you said to him?"

"Yes."

"Did you ever call for help?"

"I kicked my feet against the window a couple of times."

"Did anybody come to help you?"

"No. I saw an older couple get in their car."

"But they didn't help you?"

"No."

In the jury box and across the courtroom a grave silence fell and lingered.

"Cross-examination," Judge Long said.

"No questions, Your Honor," said Mr. Hatcher.

"Thank you, ma'am. You may step down," Judge Long said.

As I stepped down from the witness stand, I looked into the faces of the jury and saw that several of them were wiping away tears. They had seen. They knew. They finally understood what had happened to me and they realized what Hollabaugh had intended to do to Suzanne. Thank you, Jesus. "The Lord is near to all who call on Him, to all who call on Him in truth. He fulfills the desires of those who fear Him; He hears their cry and saves them" (Psalm 145:18–19).

After my testimony, the attorneys presented closing arguments to the jury.

Mr. Hatcher stayed true to form and attacked the witnesses. He said the most damning testimony came from a woman who testified as true something she only read in the newspapers, and that the second most damning testimony comes from "a man who looks like a bum who says, 'I was strung-out.'"

"We've got this screwdriver that the redneck over there found under the pickup truck. This is a man who comes to court to testify in a kidnapping case wearing cowboy boots and blue jeans and a two-day beard. What in the world do you think he looks like when he's not doing something important? What's he doing out there coming to his wife's workplace anyhow getting money from her to go buy parts for whatever rattletrap vehicle he's trying to drive."

Mr. Hatcher then said the police made a "big deal out of one palm print," and hammered the principle of reasonable doubt, saying none of it made any sense.

Mr. Brown said the crime made perfect sense. "Donald Hollabaugh ran into something that he hadn't expected. People who are willing to get involved. With Leisha Joseph, people walked by, got in their cars, left. He figured, why should things be any different in North Augusta?

"There's an old saying that the only way for evil to triumph is for good people to stand by and do nothing. That is what Donald Hollabaugh was counting on, but in North Augusta the good people didn't stand by and do nothing. Bobby, Jana, Angela, all got involved."

Mr. Brown outlined the major testimony and evidence points for the jury, then defended Bobby, saying that with adrenaline kicking in, he sensed something was wrong and grabbed Hollabaugh. And, he said, Bobby probably wore his everyday clothes to court because he didn't want to put on airs.

Judge Long called a recess and the jury went off to deliberate. I stood up and walked down the long hallway to compose myself. A little way ahead, I noticed that Judge Long was just closing the door to his chambers. He walked toward me and held out his hand.

"Leisha, I've heard about you, how you prayed for that rat for eleven years. I'm a Lutheran. I just ain't got that kinda faith, though I admire it. It's a privilege to meet you. I'm real sorry for all you've been through."

"Thank you, Judge Long. It's a pleasure to meet you. Can I talk to you for a few minutes?"

"Well, now, you know we can't talk about the case."

"I know. This isn't about the case."

"Then you come right in, step into my chambers."

I pulled the Bible from beneath my arm and placed it on his desk. He looked down and saw the name that had been inscribed.

"I'd like to give this to Donald Hollabaugh."

"So that's the gift." He looked me in the eye, winked and said, "Well, don't you worry none, honey, I'll make sure he gets it."

He handed the Bible back to me and I placed it beneath my arm. After nearly a week, it was beginning to feel like part of me. I wondered what Judge Long would do.

The jury found Hollabaugh guilty of kidnapping and assault and battery with intent to kill. Mike Terry looked at me, nodded once and smiled.

As Hollabaugh stood before the judge awaiting his sentence, you could have heard a pin drop in the courtroom. Suzanne and I were seated in the front row clinging to our families and quietly sobbing. The week had taken its toll on our emotions.

"Before I sentence you, do you have anything to say to anyone in this courtroom?" Judge Long asked Hollabaugh, obviously referring to Suzanne and me, who were openly sobbing behind him.

"I'm almost speechless, sir," Hollabaugh said. Hearing his voice for the first time in eleven years made my skin crawl.

"You know," he continued, "I worked very hard to turn my life around since 1979. Both those incidents I pleaded to in Ohio happened in the same day. There were a lot of things that were happening in my life that aren't now and I am a completely different person. I've educated myself, tried to obtain a professional job. I didn't work for nine years to get out of prison and turn my life around and come down to South Carolina and throw it all away on one Friday afternoon . . ."

Judge Long's voice boomed through the room. "I said do you have anything to say to anyone in this courtroom?"

"Judge, I told ya, I earned my degree and I got a good job. I—"

Judge Long lifted his hand in the air as if he were a beat cop halting traffic. "Shut up, that's not what I asked you." Clearly, Judge Long was disgusted.

Grief overtook me. I felt as if I were experiencing what it will be like for many before the judgment seat of Christ. Here was a judge who held this man's life in his hands. And he was being given an opportunity to show repentance or remorse, but instead he was standing proud, justifying himself with all his good works.

We were all sickened by it, especially Judge Long. Had Hollabaugh no ounce of human decency? Had he no feelings or conscience? Obviously not. What a waste of a precious moment in time.

Judge Long's voice boomed again. "Boy!" he nearly shouted. "Boy! Your mind is bent. You're brilliant, smart obviously. I don't know what in your background, sex perversion or whatever it might be, caused you to do these things. I don't know where along life's trail your mind got bent, but it's bent. Now, we have to pass judgment here. How the good Lord passes judgment on myself, you, Elmer and the rest of us, we don't know. But for mankind, I feel like I need to protect the people. You are gonna pay your debt to society, and even more so, I hope you take it up with the Lord."

Was I in a movie? Did I really hear what I just heard?

The judge continued, "Now, you see that woman right there?" And he pointed to me. "Right there, turn around and look at her! She has prayed for you for eleven years. Now, I'm a Lutheran—I just can't understand that kinda faith."

A soft laugh rippled through the room.

"She has brought you a gift and I order that you receive it. You will take it to jail with you and it must be on your person at all times."

I thought I was dreaming. God, only You could conceive of this! Vengeance is mine, saith the Lord.

Judge Long then asked Bobby to stand up.

"I commend you. I commend you, I commend you, I commend you. And I commend you. Thank God for young men like yourself. Thank God that the citizens in South Carolina and this part of the country, generally, endanger their lives to protect somebody else. There are places where people don't care, but here it's different."

Judge Long sentenced Hollabaugh to the maximum sentence he could impose: life for kidnapping, a twenty-year consecutive sentence for assault with intent to kill, and ordered that he receive psychiatric treatment.

Mr. Hatcher immediately moved that the judge set aside the jury's verdict because the state's evidence didn't support it, and for a new trial based on the grounds that I should not have been allowed to testify.

"All right," Judge Long said. "Motion denied."

"Your Honor, there is one thing I would like to ask," Mr. Hatcher said. "It is my understanding that the jail intends to take him up to the Department of Corrections as soon as they can. His mother is here from Ohio. She's quite elderly. It's virtually impossible for her to travel back and forth and this may be the last time she gets to visit him. I would like for them to have a brief period of time before they leave the courthouse, if they could do that."

As the judge hammered out the details of Hollabaugh's visit with his mother, I watched Mr. Hatcher take the Bible from the bailiff and felt a deep sense of gratification. I know there is no rehabilitation for Hollabaugh, only rejuvenation. And that is available in Christ, but he must choose it.

For me, giving Hollabaugh the Bible was part of letting go, releasing myself from the past and from all he had done to me and all that I had suffered at his hand. It was now up to him to reconcile with God. "Speaking the truth in love, we will in all things grow up in Him" (Ephesians 4:15).

I walked a little taller that day. I will always be growing in God, and the healing process is ongoing. With trauma such as I've suffered, healing is never really finished. But that day marked a high point in my recovery. I felt as if I were at least out of the hospital.

Realizing the pain that God's people were suffering, Tom and I began "Woman at the Well" ministries to help other victims. Tom went back to school and earned his master's degree in clinical Christian counseling.

The more I shared my story with others, the more the ministry grew. The needs of God's people were growing, too. We seldom saw wounded people anymore. Now we saw the traumatized. It seemed to me that in the eleven years we had been married, society had gone from wounding people to ravaging them.

We started hearing stories of satanic ritualistic abuse, child pornography and murder. There were times I could hardly bear the stories. I would ask God, how can I help these people? Lord, they've gone through so much more than I could ever dream of living through.

A man once told me of a horrendous murder in his family, and after trying to comfort him, I broke down and wept. How could that man have lived through this? Lord, what have I to offer this man? I felt the Lord speak to me in such a strong tone. Leisha, you still don't get it, do you? It's not about you, it has nothing to do with you. It's about Me, it's about the Holy Spirit, it's about *grace!* My grace applied to any given situation is sufficient. If you went through what that man did, I'd take grace and fashion it perfectly for you, just like a garment is expertly fitted for the one who will wear it.

I finally understood that God's grace covers everything. And I knew He used that illustration because I love vintage clothing. Because they are often hand-sewn to fit the lady they belonged to years ago, I delight in finding pieces that fit me.

While our work was strong, my health was not. After the trial, I began to have more health problems. I had learned that stress or pressure often brought about health difficulties for me. I believe emotional trauma spills out in many different ways, one of them through our health. The bleeding from the hemorrhage I'd suffered before my wedding had never gotten under control, and shortly after Alex was born, I'd had to have a hysterectomy. After the trial, a basal cell carcinoma was removed from my face, and I'd had two suspicious lumps removed from my breasts. I was just beginning to feel better when Tom went to the Air Force Academy in Colorado Springs to wrestle with cadets to keep in practice and had to be taken to the hospital.

The doctor took me into the darkened hospital corridor that smelled of medicines and disinfectants and told me he had to operate. Tom had a severely herniated disk and doctors had discovered during the examination that he also suffered from a congenital spine disease that had been worsening.

O God, I prayed, now what? This was Tom, my strength. Tom was a full-time pastor at Solid Rock Church, and we didn't have health insurance. It dawned on me that I could get a job. I picked up the newspaper and looked through the classified ads. Focus on the Family, which had recently moved to Colorado Springs from California, was advertising for an administrative assistant. Previous experience in a ministry preferred, the ad said. I had heard that Focus on the Family provided health insurance from the first day of hire.

I was excited as I drove to Colorado Springs, but my hopes soon deflated.

"You'll have to fill out this application," said the woman in personnel. "And I need to warn you, we've had over eight thousand applications since our move here. We'll schedule an appointment for you if your application is appropriate."

I was discouraged as I sat in a nearby restaurant, having lunch before

I went back to the hospital. All the failures of the past kept trying to insinuate themselves into my mind, reminding me of my heavy troubles, jeering that nothing ever went right. But I refused to believe that lie. I began to fight those feelings with every good word I could remember. "Whatever is true, whatever is noble, whatever is right, whatever is pure, whatever is lovely, whatever is admirable—if anything is excellent or praiseworthy—think about such things" (Philippians 4:8).

I finished my lunch and left the restaurant, but when I stepped into the bright sunlight, I realized I had forgotten my sunglasses. I chastised myself for my absentmindedness, returned to the table and began looking around. A tall, distinguished man rose from the next table.

"Have you misplaced something?"

"Well, yes. I left my sungla—Dr. Dobson!" I couldn't believe that I was talking to the founder and president of Focus on the Family.

"Yes, that was me the last time I checked. Can I help you find something?"

"My mind is somewhere else. I just left my sunglasses. You know, I just came from applying for a job at Focus on the Family."

"Really? What position?"

"An administrative assistant position, but I'd be willing to do any job, really."

He gestured to his companion at the table. "Allow me to introduce you to Mac McQuiston. Why don't you call Mac about your job?"

"Thank you, I will," I said, reaching out to shake Mac's hand. I'm sure I gave the limpest handshake in history I was so taken aback.

How amazing that I would meet Dr. Dobson just like I met Nicky Cruz. I was certain that God was arranging divine appointments as He continued to take care of me.

Within a few days I was interviewing at Focus on the Family with my soon-to-be new boss, Mark Maddox. I started out as his administrative assistant. Later, I was promoted to manager of ministry resources.

It turned out we didn't need the health insurance after all. Tom and I sought a second opinion and the specialist told us that while Tom may need surgery one day, at that time his injury could be treated with a less intrusive method. We were greatly relieved. The treatments worked and Tom recovered well.

My job at Focus on the Family was everything I'd hoped it would be. It was challenging, fun, and allowed me to be creative. It was a joy to work for such a deeply committed organization surrounded with dedicated people who were strong in Christ. Each and every workday began with devotions to God.

As part of my job, I attended many meetings, and it was at one of them that I discovered why I'd never been good at sports in high school. I had always loved to run but could never seem to catch my breath. Whenever I tried to compete, I always got smoked by Diana Huskins, the fastest girl in our high school.

During a discussion in a management meeting, I started to feel light-headed. I could see people's mouths move, but I could hear only part of what they were saying. The conversation faded in and out like bad reception from a distant radio station. The experience reminded me of the day I overdosed and came to God. Then the faces around me became blurry. It felt like my brain was short-circuiting. I knew something was terribly wrong. I left the boardroom and went straight to my doctor's office. I obviously wasn't thinking clearly. I drove myself there.

A tilt-table test revealed that I have a mild heart condition called neurocardiogenic syncope, which is controlled by medication. Doctors believe I'd had this condition for many years. Ah-ha! All my life I had been self-critical because I couldn't keep up, couldn't compete in sports, was the last one around the track. I would run a mile or two every day but never seemed to get in shape. I would become discouraged. You're just a weakling! I criticized myself. You're not trying hard enough. Negative thoughts can do so much damage. Knowledge is so powerful. It's liberating to come to the true understanding about something.

When the doctor gave me this news, I wondered if I could have beat Diana Huskins if I had been on medication in high school.

I still had other health problems. I still suffered serious headaches. And since the second trial, my screaming nightmares had worsened. I would wake up to Alex screaming in terror only to learn that it wasn't him having a nightmare, but me, and my horrible screaming had frightened him. This went on for many nights and I prayed for some relief from the horrible dreams, but relief never came.

I had always suffered from periodic nightmares. But I came to realize that some daytime trigger, such as seeing a television show where someone was shot, would cause night terrors for all of us. Tom and I would spend a great deal of time comforting Alex just so he could go back to sleep.

On the whole, though, life for us was good. Tom was a church pastor and also started working full-time at a local hospital. As a family we spent long hours together, just as I had as a kid when my dad was alive. We delighted in our Alex, who was a live wire. One of our favorite activities together was camping, and we went whenever we could. That summer we went to family church camp. One evening the adults were lingering in the dining room over coffee and dessert. The children, not ones to waste time eating, had gulped down their food and had gone outside to enjoy the last sunlight of the day.

Tom and I were quietly talking when we heard screams from across the room and saw a table full of women scatter, sending chairs flying.

Tom and I gave each other a knowing look. It must be Alex, our little mischief magnet. If there was a way to stir up excitement, Alex always found it. Women from other tables began to scream and flee from the room. Sure enough, there was Alex, heading straight for us. Just as Moses raised his staff and parted the Red Sea, Alex raised up whatever he had in his hand and parted the room. He ran through the middle of the cafeteria, sending waves of fleeing adults scrambling over chairs and tables in his wake.

"Dad! Dad! Dad! Look what I got! Can I keep it? Can I take it home? Dad!"

My heart softened for my little boy as I looked at the joy in his face. Then I saw what had struck terror in the hearts of grown women. Alex was pushing what appeared to be a snake in his father's face.

As I looked at women who were clutching their necks and putting hands over their mouths to stifle screams, I clamped my jaw shut and lowered my head so no one would see my grin. Tom took one look at me and burst out laughing. Our eyes met and I knew we were both thinking, only our son.

I leaned close to Alex's excited face and told him he must take his newfound pet outdoors.

"Why, Mom?" he asked. "Can I keep it? Mom, look, it's yellow and black and shiny!"

When I realized Alex held a salamander, a very pretty one, too, I laughed all the more. Tom and I realized dessert was over for us, and we took Alex by the hand and walked outside together.

"You can keep him, baby," Tom said, and I nodded in agreement. Tom has always called Alex "baby." I guess he will always be our baby. As Alex scampered off to show Sally the Salamander to his friends, Tom and I held hands as we sat on the cool grass to watch the sun go down behind the trees, and I thought back to camping trips long gone by. Yes, I thought, Daddy would have let me keep Sally, too.

Other than the nightmares, I didn't think about Hollabaugh too much. In January 1992 my witness protection coordinator called to tell me that Hollabaugh's appeal before the South Carolina Supreme Court had been turned down. He had appealed his conviction based on Judge Long allowing me to testify, claiming that the jury had been prejudiced. But the court ruled that the assaults on Suzanne and me were similar, and under the law, my testimony was proper.

For my part of the witness protection plan, I was supposed to move into a new house every year or so to make it more difficult for Hollabaugh to track me down. Tom and I tried that for a while, but found that the disruption to family life was too costly. Besides, God had protected me before. I was certain He would do it again.

Summer was in its final stages of glory. The August days were sunny and cloudless. Soft breezes twirled the silver-dollar leaves on the aspen trees, making the hillsides sparkle with splashes of rich gold. We were savoring the wonderful weather, knowing that soon we would be digging ourselves out from beneath piles of snow.

My nightmares had subsided. I was bewildered to wake up at 2:30 A.M. the night of August 26 from a strange dream and surprised by the peace that surrounded me. I had dreamed that I was at home alone when I heard a knock at the door. I peeked through one of the glass windows along each side of the door and saw a policeman. I opened the door, and standing there in a policeman's uniform was Donald Hollabaugh.

I sat up in bed and shook Tom until he awakened.

"He's escaped," I said. "We have to pray."

Tom didn't question. He and I knelt beside our bed and he held me as we prayed until dawn. I was certain that Hollabaugh would make good on his promise to hunt me down and kill me, but strangely I felt no fear. I felt calm, peaceful, safe.

Whom shall you fear when I am with you? asks the Lord. No one, Lord. No one.

Even after being up for most of the night, Tom and I felt refreshed as we changed our clothes and headed off to work.

I had intended to telephone my witness protection coordinator immediately, but as I entered my office, the telephone was already ringing. It was Mike Benzie, the head of security at Focus on the Family.

"Leisha, a man has been calling here looking for you, only he's asking for you by Leisha Miller. Because your first name is so uncommon, I figured he wanted you."

"That's my maiden name. Mike, you better come to my office. I have something to tell you."

I hung up the phone and it immediately rang again. It was Alex, who was home with a sitter. "Mom, some man called here for you, but when I said you were at work, he hung up. He asked for Leisha Miller."

"Thanks, honey," I said. "Don't answer the door to anyone today, okay?"

I immediately telephoned my victim witness coordinator.

"Hello, Ashley, it's Leisha."

"Leisha! I cannot believe you're calling. I was just reaching for the telephone to call you."

"And I know why," I said. "He's escaped."

"How did you know that? Who called you?"

"No one. Do you remember how I told you how God works in our lives if we let Him? Well, listen to this dream," and I explained what had happened to me the night before.

"Leisha, I don't know what to say. That's unbelievable. But you should know that we have reason to believe he's coming after you. There are some precautions you need to take."

Within minutes after I hung up the telephone, Mike arrived in my office with Dr. Dobson. My heart sank. I worried that Dr. Dobson would fear that my presence would put the other fifteen hundred employees at risk. I envisioned being immediately fired and escorted off the premises. I went through every step of shame, humiliation and embarrassment in my mind's eye.

After a few seconds, my office was filled with vice-presidents. I wanted to disappear. Lord, will my life ever be normal?

Dr. Dobson quickly assessed the situation and, like a general, took command. "You," he said, pointing to one vice-president, "call the FBI.

You," he pointed to another, "get this family on a plane and get them out of town. You, secure the staff."

As they began to move like obedient soldiers, my fear melted away.

"Leisha, don't you worry, we'll take care of everything," Dr. Dobson said.

Take care of everything? I was expecting to be fired. I was completely overwhelmed by the extent that he cared. It seemed that within minutes Tom, Alex and I were on a plane heading out of state. We stayed secluded in a wonderful home that was at our disposal for two weeks.

At about 7:15 P.M. on August 25, Hollabaugh and Donald Hallock had cut through three chain-link fences of South Carolina's Central Correctional Institute, a maximum security prison, before jumping into a waiting dark-colored automobile that was being driven by an unknown civilian. They then drove to Wilkesboro, North Carolina, where they robbed an elderly couple who operated a used-car lot. From there, the trail grew cold, but police warned me that they believed Hollabaugh was coming after me.

The police and the FBI launched a national manhunt for Donald Hollabaugh and Hallock. Hallock had been convicted of assault and battery with the intent to kill after shooting two Blackville, South Carolina, police officers. He had six prior convictions for bank robbery.

After two weeks, I insisted on going back to work. When I returned, my office had been moved to a more secure location within Focus on the Family and a security system had been installed just for me. Mike, who was a muscular six foot two inches, was under orders to guard and walk with me everywhere. Whenever I left the office, he was at my elbow. Needless to say, we became very good friends.

The entire staff was alerted to the problem and was cautioned to screen telephone calls and to keep an eye out for me and anyone who looked suspicious.

Overcome with gratitude, I went into Dr. Dobson's office. "Doctor," I said, as everyone fondly calls him, "you don't have to do this. I'm not afraid, really. You're going to a lot of expense."

He stopped me midsentence. "I want you to know that I would do this for any employee here."

"Thank you, sir," I said.

"You're quite welcome."

As I mulled over Dr. Dobson's words, I thought of Jesus' example of the lost lamb.

"If a man owns a hundred sheep, and one of them wanders away, will he not leave the ninety-nine on the hills and go to look for the one that wandered off? And if he finds it, I tell you the truth, he is happier about that one sheep than about the ninety-nine that did not wander off. In the same way your Father in heaven is not willing that any of these little ones should be lost" (Matthew 18:12–14).

God cares about each one of us, individually and specially, and when we can offer the same kind of love to others, it's like God reaching down from heaven.

The FBI provided protection for us as we awaited Hollabaugh's capture. It didn't take long. I had only been back to work a couple of days when, on September 10, Hollabaugh and Hallock led police on a high-speed chase for several miles down I-75 in Dalton, Georgia, before police boxed them in and captured them. The men had robbed a Bass shoe store on an interstate exit just before the chase.

I was relieved, but my first question to police officers was "Did he have his Bible with him?"

Of course, they didn't know. But what they did find in his wallet were the phone numbers and addresses for me and for Suzanne.

Shortly after Hollabaugh was caught, Dr. Dobson asked to hear the whole story, then asked if he could interview me for his popular national radio program. I was quite honored, but very nervous being interviewed by my boss. The doctor and the production crew worked to make me feel comfortable.

Dr. Dobson is so good at what he does. After seeing him in action like a general, I was a little intimidated and felt like I simply said "Yes" to every question he asked. I feared I wasn't a good interview for him, but prayed that the Holy Spirit would be able to use my words to touch hearts.

After the broadcast, Hollabaugh's family called Focus on the Family. On the broadcast Dr. Dobson had not revealed my identity or that I worked for him. The family wondered if Focus on the Family would put them in touch with me. I was open to the idea, but the FBI agent, Mike Terry and everyone who had worked so hard to protect me and my family were opposed.

"We don't think you should have any contact with his family," the FBI agent said. "What if they're trying to find you? We don't like it at all."

I prayed about it and approached Mike Benzie with the idea of recording the call in case any threats were made. The FBI thought that was a good compromise.

Dr. Dobson supplied a sound room with the top recording equipment available. My husband, the FBI agent, Mike Benzie and H. B. London, Dr. Dobson's cousin and head of pastoral ministries at Focus on the Family, were present. I was nervous but confident with so many there to support me.

The call was placed, but no one answered and I felt let down. Maybe this just wasn't meant to be, I thought.

"Let's try again," the sound engineer said.

After several rings a woman answered. Her voice was pleasant and calm as she told me that she was Hollabaugh's sister-in-law. Both she and her husband were Christians and had heard my testimony on Dr. Dobson's program. She said Hollabaugh had been brought up in a loving home and that the family didn't understand what had happened to him.

"We're so sorry," she told me. "We're praying for you."

"Thank you," I said. "I'm praying for your brother-in-law."

I still pray for Hollabaugh, although not every day anymore. I still pray that God will rejuvenate him and regenerate him and do for him what He's done for me. And I pray that God's justice will continue to roll down. Hollabaugh is scheduled to come before the South Carolina parole board in September 2000. Even with a mandatory life sentence for kidnapping and a prison escape on his record, our system allows him to be considered for parole after ten short years.

"It's not a matter of *if* he gets paroled, Leisha," Lawrence Brown told me in January 1998. "It's just a matter of when."

I intend to be at the parole hearing to tell my story once again before another very important audience, and without fear.

If anyone has reason to fear, it's me. I've definitely earned that right. However, today, I walk without fear. When we hold on to fear, it thwarts the very plan God has for our lives. It debilitates us and prevents us from fulfilling His divine purpose in our lives.

I travel all over the country for my business and share my story. I stay in hotels alone. I drive by myself and I never fear. There was a time I could not have done that, but through God's help and healing in my life, heart and mind, I can. Daily, I bathe myself in His Word because so many things could trigger memories. I would quickly spiral downward, but the truth of God's Word holds me upright. It protects me and defends me.

We are not given an exemption card from the world when we become a Christian. We will have tribulation, we will have trouble. The world around us is fallen, it is full of sin, crime, viciousness, the Devil, and all that he is. What we are guaranteed is that God will be with us no matter what we go through. It's a joy to live as a Christian, because God can take any heap of ashes and turn it into glory.

Hollabaugh may try to escape again, but I'm not afraid. I have faced him before, I may face him again, and if I do, God will be my defense every single time. Of that, I couldn't be more certain.

> *He who dwells in the shelter of the Most High will rest in the shadow of the Almighty. I will say of the Lord, "He is my refuge and my fortress, my God, in whom I trust." Surely he will save you from the fowler's snare and from the deadly pestilence. He will cover you with his feathers, and under his wings you will find refuge; his faithfulness will be your shield and rampart. You will not fear the terror of night, nor the arrow that flies by day, nor the pestilence that stalks in the darkness, nor the plague that destroys at midday.*
>
> *A thousand may fall at your side, ten thousand at your right hand, but it will not come near you. You will only observe with your eyes and see the punishment of the wicked. If you make the Most High your dwelling—even the Lord, who is my refuge—then no harm will befall you, no disaster will come near your tent. For he will command his angels concerning you to guard you in all your ways; they will lift you up in their hands, so that you will not strike your foot against a stone.*
>
> *You will tread upon the lion and the cobra; you will trample the great lion and the serpent. "Because he loves me," says the Lord, "I will rescue him; I will protect him, for he acknowledges my name. He will call upon me, and I will answer him; I will be with him in trouble, I will deliver him and honor him. With long life will I satisfy him and show him my salvation." (Psalm 91:1–16)*

God protected me and healed me because He loves me, and He loves you no less.

Chapter 12

THE
LONG
JOURNEY
HOME

*"He has showed you, O man, what is good.
And what does the Lord require of you?
To act justly and to love mercy
and to walk humbly with your God."*

— MICAH 6 : 8 (NIV)

I don't know whether those in heaven can see us or not, but I hope they can. If not, I can't wait to tell my dad what a great journey my life has been.

Long ago I stopped looking over the fence and believing the fallacy that others have it better. I have it no better than God Almighty planned for me and I thank Him for this journey that has been my life. Life itself is such a mysterious and wonderful gift. Any of us, in our most talented moments, couldn't create our children. We couldn't make them healthy or keep them breathing.

God gave me a mother and father who helped make me the person I am today. And I'm grateful for the time He gave me with my dad.

God gave me strapping brothers who bolstered, strengthened and protected me. No one stands above them. No one can outtalk Patch, outwork Kenny or outfight Joey. No one can outfish or outhunt any of them. Patch, my hero; Kenny, the wind beneath my wings; Joey, my challenger. If I ever got in trouble I think any one of them would move heaven and earth to get to me. I'm grateful to God for each one.

When I was small, God revealed Himself to me through snow-white clouds that floated on a sky as blue as an ocean. When I could see no beauty in life, God gave me art and pottery, and teachers who opened up their classrooms as well as their hearts. When I was lonely and friendless, He sent Jackie. When I was hurting and empty, He gave me Pastor Montei, who filled me with God's love.

Sometimes the fog was too thick for me to see His hand, but He was there even in the darkest of times. His words have lit my path. His blessings have been great and small.

He found for me the perfect husband. My Tom, who loves the Word of God, had a burning desire to understand my heart and an intense determination to see me healed. Understanding my deep wounds, God gave me a husband who is a pastor and also a clinical Christian counselor, and available to minister to me day and night. A man who stood strong next to me as we faced our adversaries, who held me through the night and prayed away the horrors that haunted my dreams. A man who would never conceive of leaving me, even though I raged against him. And one whose love called me home, even when I tried to leave him. Tom, my dearest friend, my rock.

God gave us our Alex before disease closed my womb. Tom and I had wanted a house full of children, and God blessed us with one. Alex, my daily blessing, who is both physically and spiritually strong. Whose crooked grin reminds me of someone else very dear. How could I ever doubt that God loves me when I look into his eyes? Alex, my son, my joy, my greatest gift from God.

When I needed the nourishment of spiritual peas and carrots, God sent to me a garden of women friends. Though scattered across the country, our hearts are entwined in support and love for one another.

He surrounded me with spiritual mentors and protectors. He brought to me Sam Butcher and Bill Biel in a bank lobby, Nicky Cruz in a hot tub and Dr. Dobson in a restaurant.

While a heart condition forced me to leave a job I loved at Focus on the Family, God gave me my own business marketing Christian products. He delivered me of fear, enabling me to walk alone in distant cities as I traveled for my business and my ministry.

He led me step by step through my spiritual healing, the greatest factor of all being the full realization of how very much He loves me.

God's healing hand is ever working. It was not until I began to write this book that Tom told me he had hunted for Hollabaugh so long ago, armed with a knife and deadly intent. Once that dark secret was shared, God's healing light dissolved the shadow in Tom's heart and we drew even closer in our healing.

He has given me the honor and the privilege of soothing the pain of others, as He has soothed mine. He has bestowed on me the honor of introducing many to the God of all comfort.

He taught me powerful words, then caused them to pour from my mouth and save my very life. His mighty angels stopped a bullet that was meant for me. He warns me of danger in my dreams. He has made my enemies my footstool.

He gave me a mother who made me see that I was special to God, even though she hadn't experienced it for herself yet. He recently gave me the great joy of seeing her accept Jesus Christ as her Lord and Savior.

I hope my dad can look down from heaven and hear me say, "Hey, Dad, see your grandson? He's so much like you. I can't wait until we all get home. I know there will be a great party. Thank you for showing me that life can be great. Thanks for putting me on your lap and reminding me that I'm a princess. I really feel like one now that I found out who is the King."

I'm walking with God on this journey that is my life. His Word is a lamp unto my feet. I'm counting on Him and being obedient to Him as He takes me by the hand and leads me home.

Rick Hoover, my dear friend and talented songwriter, heard my testimony in church one day and was inspired to write this song:

THIS JOURNEY

This journey that I'm on at times
Seems far too much to bear
And when my heart is aching
And it seems that You don't care
That's when Your Spirit reminds me
That I'm not in this alone.
You take me by the hand
And You lead me home.

Walk with me through this journey
Walk with me O Lord I pray
Through the fire and the flooding
And the testings of each day.
I know this path's not perfect
But it's the one You have made just for me
Lord please open up my eyes
To see what You see in me.

I know when I am weak Lord
Your strength in me's made strong.
At times I must confess
I'm not sure I can go on.
Then Your Spirit reminds me
That I'm not in this alone.
You take me in Your arms
And You carry me home.

Carry me through this journey
Carry me O Lord I pray
Through the fire and the flooding

And the testings of each day.
And when the water rises
And the fire's still ablaze
I just look into Your eyes
And I'm so amazed.